funny little human

Transform the way
you see yourself and
the ones you love

FIONA LUKEIS

First published in 2025 by Fiona Lukeis

© Fiona Lukeis
The moral rights of the author have been asserted.
This book is an Inspirational Book Writers book.

Author:
    Lukeis, Fiona

Title:
    Funny Little Human: Transform the way you see yourself and the ones you love

ISBN:
    9798340780355

All rights reserved. Except as permitted under the Australian Copyright Act 1968 (for example, a fair dealing for the purposes of study, research, criticism, or review), no part of this book may be reproduced, stored in a retrieval system, communicated, or transmitted in any form or by any means without prior written permission. All enquiries should be made to the author at fiona@fionalukeis.com.au

Editor: Emma Fletcher
Cover Design: Sarah Rose Graphic Design

Disclaimer:

The material in this publication is of the nature of general professional advice, but it is not intended to provide specific guidance for particular circumstances, and it should not be relied on as the basis for any decision to take action or not take action on any particular matter which it covers. Readers should obtain individual advice from the author where appropriate, before making any such decision. To the maximum extent permitted by law, the author and publisher disclaim all responsibility and liability to any person, arising directly or indirectly from any person taking or not taking action based on the information in this publication.

Contents

Foreword v

Dedication vii

Introduction - a letter of love from me to you 1

Chapter 1: How I got here 5

Chapter 2: Understanding your own human 11

Chapter 3: We're always in relationship 17

Chapter 4: Ground up versus top down 35

Chapter 5: Busting relationship myths and misinformation 43

Chapter 6: A simple truth—the power of a principle 53

Chapter 7: The principles of being human 57

Chapter 8: Our psychological immune system 73

Chapter 9: The link between thought and feeling 83

Chapter 10: We can't escape our humanness 97

Chapter 11: Separate realities 103

Chapter 12: The truth about compatibility 113

Chapter 13: The power of insight-based change 119

Chapter 14: The gift of deep listening 129

Chapter 15: Coming home to love 137

Chapter 16: The love ethic 149

Conclusion: You are the creator 153

What's next? 157

About the author 159

Thank you 161

Foreword

Fiona is a gem! Not only is she a wonderful human being, but she speaks and writes from the heart. And what has emerged from her in the lovely and illuminating *Funny Little Human* is wisdom that can help change lives to embody the true meaning of mental health.

The principles Fiona writes of in this book are beginning to quietly and slowly sweep the world, one bristle at a time. Those lucky enough to truly grasp this understanding of how everyone's experience of life is created moment to moment (whether we know it or not) are able to shed the past, set aside worry, anxiety and fear of the future, and totally embrace the moment to live a life full of peace, love, joy and wisdom.

Fiona Lukeis has experienced this in her own life. She knows of what she speaks and writes. She has the gift of being able to convey this understanding to others in a simple, compelling and profound way.

And to think this all started from the out-of-nowhere, spontaneous enlightenment experience of one ordinary man who found his life completely changed. Sydney Banks began talking to anyone who would listen about what he had realised for himself for the sole purpose of being helpful to humanity. Many lives began to change around him.

Those people then began to spread it to others and others and onto still others like ripples in a pond, and it has grown exponentially ever since, one person at a time, with insights of their own. Fairly early on I was lucky enough to be one of those ripples. Fiona Lukeis is one of those ripples.

Funny Little Human is a valuable link in the chain from those who came before to those who will be gratefully affected as a result of reading the treasures found herein. So sit back, relax, enjoy, allow the mind to clear, be open to the new, have no expectations and be amazed at the insights that await.

We certainly are funny little humans.

—Jack Pransky, Ph.D.
Author, *Somebody Should Have Told Us!*
Hadley, Massachusetts, U.S.A

Dedication

This book is dedicated to you, my dear reader.

You're seeking a deeper connection to life, love, and the people who matter most to you – and I want you to know that this is all possible. No matter what has happened in your past or what you may believe about yourself.

You are worthy of love. You are enough. You already hold everything you need within you.

And to my beautiful Relatable family: the loving, supportive community you've created is sending ripples of kindness, compassion, and understanding around the world. My gratitude and love for every one of you is beyond words.

Introduction – a letter of love from me to you

Dear funny little human,

Yes you, reading this book.

The first thing I want to say is that I love you. I deeply, deeply love you.

You might be thinking, *how can she say that? How can she possibly claim to love someone she doesn't know?*

I love you because we are connected. We are all connected. We are the same, you and me.

And that sameness we share is a beautiful, wonderful thing.

Loving you means loving myself and loving life, which means deeper and richer connections.

We are the same.

Beneath the limitations of our thinking.

Beneath our memories of the past.

Beneath all the things that have happened to us.

Beneath our personalities and who we think we are (and who we think we're not), we are all the same.

We come from the same place. We're made of the same elements, and we're powered by the same energy—the energy of the Universe and of creation itself. We're guided by the same fundamental principles of the human experience.

We're all different expressions of the same thing. Each expression is just as unique, powerful, and valuable as the other.

And our nature is love. Love is who we are. It's our essence. It comes already built-in within every single one of us—it's also something we all crave and search for.

There is so much joy, love, and peace within each of us, when we can see this for ourselves.

You know what else we have in common?

We're pretty funny.

Hilariously, innocently, deliciously funny. We are all in fact, funny little humans.

As human beings, we think life is a serious business. And so, we tend to take ourselves pretty seriously too. Over time, we become more rigid in our thinking, and we grow more and more attached to our own personal views and reality. We believe our reality is the only reality.

This rigidity builds an armour around our heart, our mind, and our emotions. Life starts to feel harder. We lose our sense of ease and flow. We feel a need to control ourselves, our environment, and the people around us, to feel safe. And not surprisingly, this is

Introduction – a letter of love from me to you

the point where relationships fall apart, and people get stuck. *Really* stuck.

But when we begin to see the truth of ourselves, when we start to understand the funny little humans we are, something interesting happens.

We relax. We let go. The weight lifts. Our controlling thinking falls away, and we instinctively lean into the unknown. We start to expand.

This feeling of expansion is the greatest feeling in the world. It's extraordinary. And it's so transformative for our connection, our wellbeing, and our relationships.

This is not a book about gender differences, personality types or examining wounds from the past. It's not about communication methods, attachment styles or love languages. If you're looking for a step-by-step process on how to change *x, y, z*, this is not that kind of book.

Funny Little Human is about seeing the truth of what we really are. It's about understanding the way us humans work.

Through the power of that understanding, we get to see and embrace our sameness, and see the simple, wonderful, and funny truth of our own humanity.

I want to take you beyond the limitations of your intellectual and personal mind and guide you towards the incredible power of insight and fresh thinking—the only way we create long term sustainable change.

When a human being experiences this for themselves, they get to come home.

Home to their heart.

Home to their soul.

Home to their greatness.

My deepest wish for you is that you can see this for yourself. Through understanding, nurturing, and connecting with your own funny little human.

Understanding the truth of what I really am, is the single greatest thing that has ever happened to me. It's a gift that is endlessly giving, over and over and over.

I want to help you connect with that.

Much love to you, funny little human.

Fiona x

Chapter 1

How I got here

It was 2012 and my marriage was in trouble.

My husband Sam and I were really struggling, and even though over the course of my career, I had studied just about every program on human behaviour out there, nothing seemed to be working.

I was angry, resentful, and overwhelmed. I didn't feel supported or listened to in the way I needed. In return, Sam was withdrawn and defensive, and he would often shut down. It felt like we were worlds apart and drifting further every day.

This was compounded by some very stressful life events at the time; a difficult and drawn-out custody battle with the father of my two older boys, and ongoing financial pressures following the global financial crisis that had completely wiped us out.

These stresses had me lying awake for hours night after night, stuck in a debilitating cycle of panic and overthinking. I swung between making meticulous plans to move us forward and wanting to abandon it all and run for the hills.

I had very little emotional bandwidth for life in general. My mind raced with fear and worry about the future, I was impatient with

my younger children, and I was a lot more reactionary to the small stuff. Lost car keys, a forgotten item on the shopping list, muddy footprints on the floor, would send me straight into overwhelm and resentment.

I just couldn't seem to bounce back from life's knocks like I used to—and there were plenty of those. All I could see was the impossibly high mountain I had to climb, and I felt completely alone in what I had to face.

Stuck in survival mode

For a long time, I did what many of us do in times of unrelenting stress—I told myself to 'get over it' and I just kept pushing through. Life had become one long endurance test, and I was locked in survival mode every day. There was no down time, no moment to take a breath. I was doing what I needed to do for my family, but I was totally shut down, not really feeling or experiencing any of it.

I was on autopilot at the wheel of my life, and I was drowning in overwhelm.

Deep down I knew I was taking life too seriously, and I needed to lighten up, but I had no idea how to do that. Everything was magnified and hard and impossible to solve. I couldn't work out how Sam and I had gone from being so in love to being so disconnected.

It finally came to a head one Sunday. We were in the kitchen, on a cold grey afternoon in the depths of a Melbourne winter, and we'd just had another frustrating, circular argument that went nowhere. It was like we were on different planets, and I couldn't bear it any longer. I just wanted to scream.

In the heat of the moment, I told him that I was done. I couldn't live like this, wasn't sure if I even loved him anymore, and we needed to separate. My words felt final, yet inside I was far from certain. But our differences seemed so insurmountable, and even though I was in shock, it was a relief just to say it. I thought finally there was a way out of the exhausting cycle we were stuck in.

As devastating a way out as it was.

The gift of understanding

Looking back at that moment from the perspective I now have, I feel an overwhelming sense of gratitude and appreciation.

We came so close to the brink, Sam and I, to the point of no return. But we were given a profound gift. A gift that allowed us to find each other again, to reconnect and move forward together.

This gift is a feeling beyond anything I can put into words.

It's the same profound gift I now share with my private clients and the students in my Relatable program, and I want to share with you in this book.

At the time of that crisis, Sam and I had been married around eight years. This year, as I write this book (2024), is our 20th wedding anniversary, and I can honestly say we are closer and more deeply in love than ever.

It wasn't because those external stresses just magically vanished either. We still had those mountains to climb, but we climbed them together. The goodwill, connection, and playfulness we now have, and our ability to get over stuff—without the sticky emotional residue many of us carry around for years, decades and even lifetimes—is a big part of that. We just have so much fun together. It's something I will never take for granted.

Looking back on that difficult time, through the lens of what I now know, I can see that so much of my thinking back then—even when I was drowning in all that worry, stress and resentment—was actually pretty funny. Hilarious even. My funny little human was *really good* at getting overly dramatic up on its high horse, and taking life way too seriously.

In fact, I often say to my clients and students that if self-righteousness were an Olympic sport, my human would have been up on that podium in first place with the Australian national anthem playing again and again.

I had innocently spent years honing that 'craft', not realising the impact it was having on myself, my life, and my relationships.

The power of one

We're often quick to discount something because our human mind loves to jump in with all sorts of noise and rules and opinions, and then gather all the evidence to prove it's right.

For example, you might be thinking: *What about her husband, what about his role? It looks like she's taking responsibility for everything. Here we go, another woman taking it all on board, making it their problem. Where is he in all of this?*

And this is a valid question. There are, of course, always other funny little humans we're in relationship with. And those humans bring their own unique thinking and feeling to the table. As did my husband, Sam.

But the real gift of this understanding is the extraordinary ripple effect that one person can set in motion. As you'll see in this book, as we dive deeper into this, it's not about one person doing all the work or taking all the responsibility. It's about understanding how the human experience is created and the power this has to transform every relationship in our lives.

Back then, my little human (and my husband's) was doing the best it could at the time. It didn't have the understanding I have now, of how human beings work, how life works, and who it really was underneath all that insecure thinking. Even though I'd 'done the work', there were fundamental, spiritual principles about what it is to be a human being that were missing.

Once I learned about these principles, everything changed. I had the privilege of getting to know and understand my own funny, quirky, and intense little human through a lens of humility, playfulness, love, and grace.

The impact of this has rippled out around me, to my husband, my children, my family, and friends. And it has travelled beyond, to the hearts and minds of people around the world, people I don't even know, yet feel a deep connection to.

This is the power that's on offer. The power of one person to create transformational change.

A quick note: *If you haven't yet read the 'Introduction - a letter of love from me to you' at the start of the book, I recommend pausing here to do that now. It's an important starting point and sets the stage for what I'm going to share with you in this book.*

Chapter 2

Understanding your own human

"The one constant in life is change."
- Heraclitus

By her own admission, Alice was a planner.

With her small business, she thrived on being organised and planning ahead. She had a clear vision of how things should be—in her business, her friendships, and her life—and when everything ran the way she wanted, she felt calm and happy.

One thing Alice didn't thrive on was change, and lately despite her best efforts, life was not sticking to the plan. Her teenage son, Alex, was growing fast. He'd started challenging any request, barely grunted hello, and would disappear into his room as soon as he got home.

Things were also changing with her best friend. Rachel used to call Alice every day but now seemed distant and preoccupied with a new relationship. Even Alice's business, which usually brought her such joy and satisfaction, had become difficult with increasing requests for refunds and a drop in sales. No matter how hard she worked, she couldn't seem to get things back on track.

Alice was feeling overwhelmed by so much changing all at once. It left her worried and frustrated, and the more she tried to control everything, the more out of control it all felt.

The nature of change

We all know that change is a natural part of life. But despite the absolute certainty and inevitability of it, we human beings are not terribly fond of change. In fact, we tend to avoid it like the plague. Most of us prefer to stay in our little comfort zones (even when we're not so comfortable). We like things to be a certain way—and to stay that way, thank you very much.

When change does come, we often find ourselves locked in the brace position, kicking and screaming in outright protest, or in complete denial. Rarely do we meet it head on.

How often have you heard of someone in shock when their long-suffering partner leaves: *I knew they weren't happy, and they wanted us to get counselling, but I didn't really think things were that bad.*

Or someone stuck in a job they hate: *I know I'm miserable and bored, but it pays the bills, and I don't know if I can get another one.*

Or someone with a friend who always brings them down: *She's always criticising my choices. I need to set better boundaries with her, but I don't want to upset the friendship.*

That innocent human inside us all wants things to stay the same to keep us safe, even when we know things could be better. I've been there myself; my own little human has resisted change many, many times.

When life throws us something unexpected, our human often gets frightened, overwhelmed and reactionary. Because it takes life so seriously, change is seen as a threat.

Once this happens, we get stuck. Stuck in our thinking, stuck in our reality, stuck in our fears. And our funny little human starts really overcomplicating things, creating more overthinking, more overwhelm and more fear. We then say or do things we don't mean, having a classic Homer Simpson 'Doh!' moment. Because once that emotional fog lifts, we can't believe we did or said those horrible things we didn't mean.

But here's the good news.

The more we understand our funny little human, the easier it is to let ourselves (and others) off the hook. We learn how to 'get over ourselves'. We put down the heavy, exhausting load we're carrying, and we start leaning into all the good stuff that life has to offer.

The more we understand ourselves, the more resilient we become to our own insecure thinking. The more we embrace the truth of who we are, the more connected, energised, and alive we feel. We get to experience a depth of feeling that is much deeper, richer, and more potent than we can possibly imagine.

And best of all, it's not as dependent on what's happening outside of you as you might think. Once you see and experience the truth of the 'inside out' nature of your experience, it will truly set you free. And that freedom lies in letting go, not holding on tighter. The more space we allow, the greater the peace, calm and emotional bandwidth we have access to.

For Alice, this idea of letting go felt dangerously radical, as though she was freefalling. She had a lot of 'what ifs', and her funny little human resisted, fearing she'd lose everything. But deep down, Alice knew that her rigid expectations were suffocating her relationships and her own happiness. She was sick of feeling so burnt out and overwhelmed.

When her son Alex was late home, Alice resisted the urge to demand where he'd been. Instead, she asked him how his night

had gone. At work, she started to delegate tasks she once thought only she could do. And she reached out to her friend Rachel with understanding instead of resentment, asking how she was adjusting to her new relationship.

These small shifts were incredibly freeing for Alice. Pressures at work eased, she found herself more productive even though she was working less. In fact, to Alice's surprise, the less she tried to control, the more connected she felt to the people around her.

Her relationship with her son softened, and even though he was still spending a lot of time in his room, she found he would suddenly appear while she was making dinner and volunteer details about his day.

Her friend Rachel confided that she'd been hesitant to call, thinking Alice was "too busy to want to know about her silly relationship issues", which led to a heartfelt reconnection between them.

As Alice's funny little human learned to release its grip on control, she discovered a whole new rhythm in her life—one that was more forgiving and joyful. She stopped seeing change as a threat to avoid, but as a natural part of life to embrace. In letting go of her need to control every detail, Alice found a freedom within herself and her life that she'd never thought possible.

We are a soul first

For many of us, we think life is all about being human first, with the soul coming a distant second, if at all.

This misconception leads to human beings who takes themselves and life very seriously. Who feel the need to control everything, and who find it hard to embrace change, let go of the past and step into the unknown. And so, they keep getting stuck, and they keep repeating the same circular pattern.

Understanding your own human

The truth is actually the other way round. We are spiritual beings having a human experience on Earth. We are a soul first, and a human second.

We can either keep repeating the same patterns in our life, or we can evolve through them. And one creates a very different experience of life than the other.

As you begin to see that life is about the soul first, you'll start to see that your funny little human is simply a vehicle for your soul's expression. You'll be able to embrace your fears, your insecurities, and your funny quirks that make you so uniquely you and allow your human to evolve and grow.

There is magic to be found everywhere in life when you're able to do this.

Chapter 3

We are always in relationship

When Emily first reached out to me, she sounded defeated. "My husband Greg and I are barely speaking, and I don't know how to fix it." She paused before adding, "It's not just him. It's me. It's always been me. I'm terrible at relationships."

Because of her past experiences and breakups, Emily had been carrying this story that she was bad at relationships around with her for years. Now, on the brink of separating from her husband, it felt like all her worst fears about herself were confirmed.

But while Emily had come to me about her struggles with her husband and their marriage, it became clear the issue went much deeper. Emily wasn't just in conflict with Greg, she was in conflict with herself.

Emily would anxiously replay their conversations in her mind, dissecting every word, convinced she'd done something wrong. If Greg seemed quiet after dinner, she'd interpret it as disapproval. "He must be tired of me," she'd think, "What did I say this time?"

This relentless self-criticism was the lens through which she viewed her marriage and the world. Instead of seeing Greg's occasional silence as a natural part of being human, Emily perceived it as a personal failing. Her hyper-vigilance eroded the easy connection

they once shared. Laughter was replaced by tension, and spontaneity gave way to self-monitoring. The harder Emily tried to be the 'perfect' partner, the more distant Greg seemed to become.

"I feel like I'm losing him," she said. "But honestly, I think I lost myself a long time ago."

Being good at relationships is a skill we can learn

Relationships are at the heart of everything we do. They impact our wellbeing, and the level of connection we have. The amount of money we make. How quickly we let go of the past, and how present we are in the now. They impact how we deal with life, especially when life 'hits'. Our relationships impact our state of mind, our mental and emotional bandwidth, and our health. They're vital for our survival.

So it makes sense that we learn how to do them well.

Being good at relationships is less about external actions, and more about building our capacity to look inside ourselves. It's having the humility to recognise there are things we all need to learn, and then making a commitment to grow within ourselves so we can show up with kindness and compassion.

I often say that being good at relationships is an essential life skill—a skill anyone can learn. And no, it's not the hard task you might be thinking. In fact, I'm going to show you just how simple, easy, and effortless relationships can be.

Hardwired for love and connection

The potential to be great at relationships is something we already have. It's in our nature, at the very core of who we are. It's our birthright to connect and experience love, joy, and wellbeing—and to give and share this with others.

It's not something we can lose either; it can't be reduced by past experiences, old wounds, or the actions of others—although to our funny little human, it sure looks that way sometimes. The truth is, we're born hardwired for connection, joy, and love, it's our true nature.

We come into this world ready and eager to connect. But as we grow up, we often lose access to this, and we drift further and further away from our own truth. To come back to this, is simply a matter of remembering and understanding who and what we already are.

What you discover for yourself in this process, applies to everyone too. This means you can take what you learn here into every single relationship you have and witness the impact of the lightness you bring and the insights you experience.

I've had clients from all walks of life—CEOs and stay-at-home-parents, bankers and business owners, tradesmen and athletes, even children—experience a profound change in how they see the world, and in what they're able to generate and create with that new understanding.

The three key relationships

In every moment of every day, there are three key relationships that are constants in our lives. The quality of these relationships directly impacts the quality of our lives, and the life of every human being on the planet.

1. Your relationship with you
2. Your relationship with life
3. Your relationship with others

There may be times when one may be more in focus than another, but we're always in relationship with all three, all the time. And in turn they all impact and flow into each other.

It's your relationship with you and your relationship with life that determines the quality of your relationship with others. When we're only looking at our relationship with others, we're missing a vital piece of the relationship skills puzzle.

The most important thing you can do for yourself right now, is to commit to doing relationships well. The moment you make that commitment, irrespective of what's happened in your past or what's going on in your life right now, you open the door to an emotional and spiritual freedom that will change your life forever.

1. Your relationship with you

It's not by chance that this relationship is number one. It's the most important, fundamental relationship you will ever have. Everything in your life flows from the relationship you have with yourself.

How you relate to yourself affects every aspect of your life. It affects how you navigate your own emotions and your own thinking. How comfortable you are in your own skin, the way you listen, how open you are, the energy you bring each day, and how you receive from others.

The lens through which you listen and filter the world is all impacted by the relationship you have with yourself.

When someone is comfortable in their own skin, they have more capacity for compassion, kindness and understanding. They're more playful, loving, and lighthearted. They move through life with a sense of humility. They know they're not perfect, and they don't expect to be. They don't expect others to be perfect either.

When someone has a good relationship with themselves, they also tend to be great listeners. They don't feel the need to prove, justify or defend themselves. They're not trying to hide who they are and as a result, they're open-minded and receptive to differences.

They also don't take life and other people so personally, which means they have more emotional bandwidth when stuff happens. They find it easier to let go and get over things quickly.

Someone who is comfortable with themselves has so much more on offer, mentally and emotionally. They're not grappling and reacting in the moment to everything that doesn't go their way.

They tend to have a good sense of humour; they can see the lighter side of life. Their energy is open and inviting, and other people feel drawn to them because their energy makes others feel emotionally safe. They champion others. They're comfortable with people around them succeeding because they don't see life or others as a competition.

Their human doesn't feel the need to people-please, they don't need everyone else to be okay so they can be okay. They set natural boundaries and they're okay to say no; their wellbeing doesn't depend on the opinion of somebody else. They're able to speak their own truth and honour who they are.

A kindness shift

As Emily started to soften in her relationship with herself, something remarkable happened.

She could see that her struggles with Greg weren't isolated, they were part of a larger story about how she related to herself and the world around her. She began to see how her inner critic—her relentless, judgemental voice—was colouring everything; her relationship with Greg, her perception of life, and even her ability to experience joy.

Emily began to let go of the idea that she had to 'prove' her worth as a partner. And in doing so, found herself showing up differently in her marriage. Instead of stewing over Greg's silence during dinner one night, Emily asked gently if he was okay. Greg looked up, surprised. "Yeah, just a rough day at work," he said, his voice tired but warm.

For the first time in years, Emily didn't interpret his mood as a reflection of herself. Instead, she saw it for what it was—Greg's own unique experience, separate from her. "That moment changed everything," she later told me. "It was so simple, but I finally felt like I could just… be with him. I didn't need to fix anything or figure out what I'd done wrong."

As Emily's relationship with herself began to shift, so did her relationship with her husband. As she learned to approach life with less judgement and more curiosity, she found herself reconnecting not just with Greg but with many simple joys she'd overlooked for years.

This transformation didn't require her husband to change. It didn't require Emily to 'fix' anything about herself. All it took was for her to see the relationships that had always been there—and to approach them with kindness, patience, and understanding.

For Emily, this shift wasn't just about improving her marriage. It was about reclaiming the fullness of her life.

The power of a good feeling

This is the impact our funny little human can have in the world when we have a good relationship with ourselves. We emit an energy or frequency that bypasses our ego or intellectual mind, and connects with others, soul to soul. We can be a force for light and good in the world, though never at the expense of ourselves.

The wonderful thing about being comfortable in your own skin, is that it makes you feel good, and this good feeling makes it easy to naturally honour who you are. We can experience a higher level of mental, emotional, and spiritual wellbeing simply because we feel good.

This is why the relationship you have with yourself is so important. And it's often one that we take for granted and don't look at enough, at least not through a lens that is empowering and inspires our own growth and expansion.

Looking through a self-critical lens

Like Emily, we often look at ourselves through a critical and judgemental lens, focused on our flaws or what we think is missing. For some, there might not be any self-awareness at all. They're simply moving through life, trying to get through the day as best they can. As a result, our relationship with ourselves can be our biggest blind spot, and our funny little human can unintentionally get way off track.

When we're off track, we can start acting in a way that's not kind or generous to ourselves and others. We can be self-absorbed and emotionally stingy. We start developing a high tolerance for being judgemental, upset, or dissatisfied, to the point that we don't even notice it anymore. When this happens our self-awareness of how we're showing up is virtually non-existent.

With a lack of self-awareness, we inadvertently keep generating more of the same, all the while wondering why the same situations keep happening to us.

Once we normalise a feeling or experience, we no longer see the edges of it, and it becomes less visible to us. In order to notice those edges again, we must be in a high state of that feeling or experience. For example, if you've ever experienced anxiety, then you'll find that over time you don't notice how anxious you are until you're in a heightened state of anxiety.

A fast and busy mind

The problem here is that in a heightened state of any emotion, our ability to do something differently in the moment is greatly diminished. So, the capacity for our human to choose something else is simply not there.

It's similar to driving a car, and a dog suddenly runs out onto the road in front of you. If you're driving at 40 km/h you have time and space to make a choice; you can safely brake or take evasive action. But if you're driving at 80 km/h, you're going too fast to have any safe, effective choices, and chances are you will hit the dog.

When we develop a high tolerance for being in a feeling like anger, sadness, criticism, suspicion, or anxiety, our intellectual mind is going so fast this barely registers. We're so busy engaging with all the content in our head that justifies that feeling, our mind is racing. And a fast, busy mind will always be more entrenched in a feeling than a calm, quiet mind that's operating at a slower pace.

By the time our human realises we're even angry, we're already beyond the capacity to choose something else. We're going too fast. And without the insight or awareness of how we're showing up, we keep repeating the same thing, wondering why nothing externally really changes.

The gift of choice

What I'm going to share with you in this book will give your human the precious gift of that awareness—and with it the invaluable gift of choice. I had a student join my program Relatable recently, and she told me, "You know Fiona, my husband really should be the one doing this as he is so uptight. I'm the calm one, nothing much tends to bother me."

After completing the first module, she sent me an email, incredulous at some of the realisations she'd had about herself. "Oh my goodness, Fiona," she wrote, "I have just discovered I am *so not the calm one!* I'm nowhere near as calm as I thought I was, I'm quite shocked at what I have missed in the way I handle things."

If you can relate to this, you're not alone, and it's not your fault. You haven't been shown a practical and empowering way to look inside yourself for the answer. As a rule, we're not taught how human beings actually work, so our funny little human can be totally clueless about how it's showing up and the impact it's having.

When we understand the spiritual principles behind being human, we develop a much higher awareness of ourselves. We have access to the precious gift of choice, and we naturally become a lot more comfortable in our own skin.

This means there are fewer mentally draining things for our human to grapple with, and more room for it to simply show up to life and be present in the moment.

The gift of awareness

This awareness is something I am so grateful for. It's become my life's work, mission, and purpose to share this gift with as many human beings as possible. Every single one of us deserves the right to get to know ourselves outside of the limitations of our own thinking. It's one of the most empowering and liberating things we will ever do.

When we have this experience, our human really gets a true sense of itself. What lights it up, what makes it feel good, what it feels like to be home within itself, and everything in between. I call this 'getting to know the shades of you', because when you get to know yourself, a lot of the overthinking and wondering we have about ourselves, and others simply falls away. There is so much less to think about.

With less on our minds, we have the space and opportunity to show up to the people we care about, in ways we never knew we were capable of.

When you begin to recognise your own greatness, when you start to honour yourself and others from this place, there are no limits to the profound impact you can have. The ripple effects of this are truly extraordinary.

That's how powerful you are.

2. Your relationship with life

Next is the relationship we have with life itself.

Our relationship with life is important because it impacts the ease with which we move through it. It affects how quickly we get over things when they don't go our way, and the belief and faith we need to face our challenges. It also affects how much gratitude and appreciation we can experience.

If you want to form deeper connections with the people you care about, if you want to be in a consistent state of wellbeing and create change in your life, the ability to look at life through a lens of gratitude and appreciation is essential.

Like our relationship with ourselves, we often overlook our relationship with life and take it for granted. It simply doesn't occur to us to look at this. So, what do I mean by your relationship with life? First, let me ask you a few questions.

How do you relate to life?

Option 1

- Do you believe that things always work out?
- Do you trust that the Universe has your back?
- Do you have a deep sense of knowing that things will be okay, even when you don't know or can't see how?
- When you want something but can't see what the next step is, do you trust that the answer will come to you?

Option 2

- Do you think that life is hard, and that no matter how hard you try life never really gives you a break?
- Do you feel like you've lost faith in life, that things never work out?

- Do you feel like you're always on guard so that the past does not repeat itself?
- Do you feel like it's you against the world and that you're out here on your own, paddling against the tide?

Take some time to reflect on this.

A quick note: Reflection is a state of mind where we allow our conscious thoughts to relax, making space for fresh thinking, new ideas, insights, and wisdom to emerge. To reflect is to try something on without searching for the right answer.

Do you relate more to the questions in Option 1 or Option 2?

If you answered yes to the questions in Option 1, this indicates that your relationship with life is very healthy and you have a deep trust in something bigger than yourself. You tend to handle change and uncertainty well.

If you answered yes to the questions in Option 2, this indicates your relationship with life needs attention.

When we don't have a great relationship with life, we're more likely to be closed off to possibilities. We're more likely to be focused on the negative than the potential. We're going to be wary of people and their motives. We tend to look at life through a lens of suspicion and worry.

We're also likely to find it hard to let go of the past or take risks. We constantly fret about the future so we can be prepared for the worst, making it harder to relax and be in the now.

When we don't have a great relationship with life, we have less trust and a greater need for control. As our need for control grows, our world gets smaller and smaller.

Learning to trust in life

A client of mine, Jess, had always felt alone. After experiencing abandonment as a child, Jess had an established belief that life wasn't fair, and it was her against the world. As she got older and had a family of her own, this belief grew stronger until her entire focus was on controlling and managing everything around her.

Dinner had to be on the table at 5 pm every day in case she got too tired and found it hard to cope. If anything derailed this strict routine, Jess would get anxious, and then get anxious about being anxious. Everything was about managing her environment so she could be okay.

Jess began to learn about the principles of being human, and a life changing moment came when she finally understood, with a deep knowing, that the Universe (or life) had her back. She wasn't on her own.

Jess said it was so liberating to feel her fear-based thinking finally begin to fall away. She learned to let go of the need to control, and start trusting in life, *even when things didn't go according to plan*. If dinner was late, if the kids weren't in bed on time, if something unexpected showed up, she knew fundamentally she would be okay. Her relationship with life completely changed, and as a result her whole world opened up.

When we don't have a great relationship with life, we think it's all up to us. We think we need things to be a certain way so we can feel safe, secure, and okay. It means we don't cope so well with change or when things don't go as planned, reducing our emotional bandwidth and resilience.

Life throws curve balls

As the philosopher and author Sydney Banks, who discovered the Principles, once said, "Life is a contact sport". No matter what we do or how hard we work, life will always throw curve balls our way, because that's the nature of life itself.

When we don't deal well with the unexpected, when we need life to be a certain way to feel okay, we tend to take life and everything it throws at us very personally. It can look as though the whole world is against us.

We're not as emotionally available to the people around us. We tend to lead with our insecurities, and we hold ourselves back from bringing the fullest expression of what we can offer.

If you have a belief that you're unlucky and things don't go your way, if you can't trust that things will work out and life does not have your back, you'll cling to the past and worry about the future. You'll find it hard to be in the present moment.

When our human feels that way, it tends to take life pretty seriously. It stops having fun and things can seem very hard and heavy. Our human will lead with its insecurities, holding itself back from the fullest expression it can offer. Our ability to connect with others is diminished because our hearts are guarded and closed, making it harder to see the beauty, joy, and other gifts in the world.

Do you see how your relationship with you, and your relationship with life, each play a vital role in how you show up to and experience life?

Can you begin to see the enormous impact they have on how deeply and authentically you connect with others?

The lens of gratitude and appreciation

When we have a good relationship with life, we have a greater sense of gratitude, joy, and abundance. We don't need to make a list of everything we're grateful for to remind us, we're already in a natural state of appreciation and gratitude.

Not long after my relationship with life changed, from one of fear and lack to one of trust and faith, I was sitting on my back deck, having a snuggle with my dog, Arlo. My house sits on a hill that looks toward a nearby mountain, and I love to sit out on the deck, soak in the view and let my mind wander.

It was mid-afternoon, I was enjoying a cup of tea, and my mind was quiet. Out of nowhere, a beautiful and spontaneous feeling of gratitude for this moment, this simple everyday moment, washed through me.

It was so strong, it sent tingles up and down my spine. I felt my heart swell and expand in response.

This was quickly followed by a feeling of gratitude for the feeling of gratitude I had just experienced! I can really only describe it as a moment of pure contentment that arose out of nowhere with no effort required to feel it.

And I thought to myself, *Wow, the lens I look at life through has really changed!* Changed to the point where gratitude is something I no longer need to remind myself to search for, it's a feeling I live in now.

If you could choose to spend time with someone who felt gratitude and joy, who frequently saw the beauty in the world, or someone who saw life as hard, unfair and complicated, which would it be?

The difference is a person with an open mind and an open heart, who naturally honours themselves, and is comfortable saying no when they need to.

A person who is more discerning about their thinking and doesn't take themselves too seriously. A person who is calm, grounded, and present, and doesn't need to micromanage or be on guard all the time, just so they can be okay.

And because of this, they're more open emotionally, mentally, and spiritually. This openness enables them to look at life through a lens of compassion and understanding, making it easier for them to let go and put their 'stuff' down. In short, they're good at getting over themselves.

Who would you rather spend time with?

3. Your relationship with others

The third key relationship is the one we have with others.

The quality of the relationships we have with the people in our lives is directly connected to our sense of significance, self-worth, and belonging.

As the English poet John Donne once famously wrote, "No man is an island". Centuries later, these words are recognised around the world as they speak to a truth about us all. Everything we do and feel flows from the quality of our connections with others.

As human beings we want to know that we matter, that we have something of value to contribute. We want to know that we belong. This is what gives us a sense of purpose and meaning. It's why connection is such a powerful and primal need within us all.

We're a part of the whole

We see a reflection of ourselves in the people we care about. We see our worth in their words, their expressions, and their actions. We place meaning on what we experience from the people around us, that meaning helps shape our personality and view of the world.

This is because human beings are hardwired for connection. You only need to look at the face of a newborn baby to see the truth of this. We come into this world innately connected and plugged into the whole.

We're designed to seek and experience love. To see love reflected in another person's eyes, heart and actions is one of the greatest feelings in the world. How we connect with others can make or break the quality of our entire lives.

The truth is we need each other. As Donne also wrote, we are "a part of the main". We are part of the whole sea of humanity and our need to connect to this is met through our relationships with others.

When we feel separate from the whole, we have a far greater sense of suffering (no matter what our situation is) than those who feel connected, accepted, and plugged into it.

That's why there is so much dialogue and discussion out there about relationships. We're all looking for the same answers. *Do I fit in here? Do I belong? Am I enough? Am I loved?*

It's why I'm so passionate about this work. Apart from our physical health, nothing else has the impact on our lives like the quality of our relationships. Especially the ones in which we have the most emotional investment.

Nothing else gives our human the same opportunity to grow and expand emotionally, mentally, and spiritually as our close, intimate relationships. This is where we can let our guard down, where we can allow ourselves to be truly 'seen'.

The impact we have on others

A dear friend of mine, Anthony, has an amazing ability to make people around him feel seen and acknowledged. Even complete strangers he meets on the street. I call this Anthony's magic.

Anthony radiates a warm, kind, and loving energy. He's genuinely interested in whoever he's talking to, and so people are naturally drawn to him. Their defences fall away, their natural state emerges, and they open up and connect with him. I've watched this unfold many times and it always blows me away.

Recently, we went away on a trip together. During the flight, I left my seat to go to the bathroom and stretch my legs. When I returned, Anthony's seat was empty. I smiled to myself, knowing he was no doubt off talking to someone he'd just met.

Sure enough, a few minutes later, one of the air stewards approached me and asked if I was travelling with Anthony. When I said yes, he immediately handed over a pile of complimentary gifts and toiletries and said, "We normally give these to our Platinum customers, but we want you and Anthony to have them. We *love* Anthony."

A week later, on our return flight home, many of the same cabin crew were on the plane. As we stepped aboard, their faces lit up and they gave us a big welcome, saying, "We were *so* excited to see Anthony's name on the passenger list today, welcome aboard!"

Anthony's magic had done it again.

Allowing more ease and flow

Through the course of my work, I've seen how people who have great relationships with others tend to find life infinitely easier in every way.

There's an ease in the way they move through life, and how they handle the big stuff, the unfair stuff, the moments when life doesn't go their way. They lean into their connections with others, and they draw strength from the people around them.

People who have strong connected relationships with others tend to be more confident, relaxed, and present. They also tend to be good listeners, and it's the ability to listen well that is the lifeblood of any relationship.

They're also able to navigate their own emotions and they're less rigid in their thinking and views of the world. They tend to have a higher level of awareness of the space they're coming from, and a natural curiosity about the world.

If they're comfortable in their relationships with themselves and with life, they're also naturally present, grounded and calm. They radiate an energy that makes the people around them feel emotionally safe. This makes them great partners, leaders, parents, siblings, colleagues, and friends.

This is why being great at relationships is an essential life skill. It's not something we can afford to ignore or limit ourselves around. It matters, and it matters to us all.

If you want to improve your relationship with you, if you want to have a different relationship with life, if you want to feel safe and secure in your relationships with others, this is what it's all about.

My intention for you is that through learning the spiritual principles of being human, your relationship with your own funny little human will transform. And in turn, bring simplicity, clarity and hope to you and the ones you love.

When enough people see this and experience this for themselves, it will change the world.

Chapter 4

Ground up versus top down

When Lily and Mark first came to see me, they were at their wits' end.

Together 14 years, they'd been struggling for the last five. They'd tried every relationship fix they could think of: regular date nights, self-help books, as well as therapy sessions focused on 'improving communication'. But despite all their efforts, the couple felt more disconnected than ever.

Date nights, which were supposed to bring them closer, often ended in awkward silence or an argument over small things. Instead of feeling romantic, they felt like they were just going through the motions or walking on eggshells to avoid another fight.

They'd even tried to understand each other better by doing quizzes and reading up about personality types and relationship styles. While this helped them to see their differences, it left Lily and Mark feeling even more stuck. "It's like we'd put each other into boxes," Lily said. "But knowing our 'types' doesn't seem to change anything. We're still not connecting."

The more they tried to 'fix' their relationship, the more complicated it became. "We're doing everything we're supposed to," Mark said. "But instead of getting closer, we feel further apart."

Building a strong foundation

It was clear their well-intentioned efforts were only adding pressure to their relationship. Without understanding the deeper source of their disconnection, these gestures were backfiring, leaving them feeling even further apart.

This is where understanding how to build a relationship from the ground up versus the top down comes in.

When we build something from the ground up, we create a solid foundation for our funny little humans to come back to again and again, irrespective of what's going on around us.

Foundations support us and ground us. They provide a secure base from which we can reflect and let go, return to, and move on from. Having a foundation of understanding in our relationships stops us from free falling emotionally. It frees our analytical mind from continually searching for a solution.

When the foundations are strong, the container of that relationship feels strong. It may get buffeted around from time to time but it remains intact.

Most traditional relationship advice, however, is more focused on building a relationship from the top down. What does that mean exactly? Top down refers to external solutions, techniques, strategies, and models aimed at 'fixing' us and our relationships.

When we focus more on prescriptive solutions, such as date nights, personality types, and aligned values, we're building from the top down. These solutions may seem promising on the surface, but they're based on the belief that how we feel in a relationship is determined by our external environment. The truth is quite the opposite.

Our experience of any relationship is created from the inside out.

I'll expand more on what I mean by this throughout the book. But basically, when we look to our external environment for answers, our human tends to focus more on differences and problems, which lowers our spirits and has us noticing only what's missing.

The 'date night' fix

Let's take the common relationship cure-all, the date night. If you're not feeling connected to your partner, going out on a date and spending time together sounds like a great idea, right?

But, as with Lily and Mark, what if there's a well of underlying resentment between you that hasn't been dealt with? You book the restaurant, organise the babysitter, get dressed up, sit down nervously at the table, and then struggle with what to say to each other.

Maybe you're still thinking about last week's argument and so you're a bit quieter than normal. Maybe your partner thinks you're not making enough effort. You're both feeling the pressure to have a good time and make it all better, but with no solid foundation of understanding between you, tension and insecurities rise. Predictably, an argument breaks out.

If the date night ends badly, which at this point looks likely, it's added to the pile of evidence of how the relationship is not working and how little you have in common.

Without the deeper foundation of understanding how human beings work, how similar we all are, and how we create our reality, all this 'evidence' can easily compress into a pressure cooker situation waiting to explode.

Personality types

Working out what 'personality type' you are is another example of building a relationship from the top down.

Personality types tend to categorise people into specific types or traits. While this may provide some surface-level observations, it can also lead to rigid opinions on how we see ourselves and others.

Personality types are often based on external behaviours, preferences, and traits, suggesting that these define who we are. When we attach these kinds of labels to ourselves or our partners, our funny little human can inadvertently miss the possibility for growth and change.

How many times have you heard the phrase 'a leopard never changes its spots'? While this might be true for some people, it's certainly not the case for the majority. I've had the privilege of seeing first hand, thousands of people who have experienced deep and lasting change as their awareness and understanding has shifted.

By focusing on personality types, we risk not seeing a deeper truth. That our experience of love, connection, and conflict comes from our thinking in the moment, not from our partner's traits or behaviours. This keeps us stuck in the idea that change in a relationship can only happen if people 'fix' their personality, instead of first recognising what it is we're each bringing to the table.

Most people tend to think in terms of how life is meeting them, instead of how *they* are meeting *life*.

When we approach a relationship from the top down, it reinforces the belief that our happiness and how we feel are solely dependent upon something external to us. This can be problematic when it comes to dealing with the gamut of emotions our funny little human must navigate through in its relationships.

Here's an example. You're looking at personality types, and you learn that your partner is more introverted than you are. On the surface this sounds like a handy thing to know, and to some extent it is. It means you can recognise how and when your partner needs to recharge, and in a healthy frame of mind you can see this and give them the space they need.

But what if you're not in a healthy frame of mind?

The human experience is constantly fluctuating, and with it our levels of emotional intelligence and insight. What if you're not in a great head space and you're taking everything personally? You might think your partner is being *too* quiet and reserved, and that it's somehow directed at you. With this thinking, you might start to feel like this is a big difference between you, and suddenly it becomes an issue.

Why can't they be more outgoing? They know I enjoy being around people and that it's important to me. I would have thought if it's important to me, they would make more of an effort. It's obvious they don't really care about me or understand me.

If you haven't learned to first look at how you're meeting the situation or how to navigate your own emotions, you can see how quickly and easily resentment can start brewing.

Aligned values

Values are another common way of looking at a relationship from the top down. When seen as fixed core beliefs that define who we are and how we should behave, values can create a sense of inflexibility in our relationships, where our humans may feel that their values need to align perfectly to be compatible. In fact, our funny little humans can get *really* hung up on whether or not they share the same values.

When we focus too much on values, we tend to judge others based on whether they share similar beliefs. In relationships, this can create an unnecessary sense of separation or division, as people often think, *We don't share the same values, we're obviously incompatible.*

Seeing values as something fixed and finite can limit us from seeing the possibility for change and growth. The truth is, our values can shift as our level of consciousness evolves, and our human sees life from a different perspective. By viewing values as unchangeable and carved in stone, we become closed off to this possibility.

Values also often come with a moral or ethical viewpoint, where certain values are considered 'right' and others 'wrong'. This rigid mindset can lead to conflict in relationships because our human feels that its values are more correct or important than the values of someone else.

We might ask ourselves:

- Do we prioritise similar things like family, career, or personal growth?
- How do we each define honesty, trust, and respect?
- Do we resolve conflict the same way?
- How do we feel about money, social connections, and life goals?
- What moral or ethical beliefs do we share?

As Lily and Mark gained this understanding, something began to shift. They started to let go of the pressure to 'fix' their relationship with external actions, and instead focused on building a foundation of empathy and trust.

One evening, instead of another date night, they decided to stay in and just talk, without any expectations. Lily noticed how much lighter the conversation was when she wasn't trying to orchestrate the perfect evening. Mark realised he could relax and be himself without the fear of saying the wrong thing.

They began to see that their connection didn't come from fancy dinners or clever communication techniques—it came from simply being present with one another, allowing space for their humanity to show.

This newfound understanding became their anchor. It didn't mean their challenges disappeared overnight, but they no longer saw tough moments as proof of a failing relationship. Instead, they saw them as opportunities to reconnect—to step back, let go of judgement, and remember the love that had always been there beneath the surface.

As Lily and Mark continued to deepen their understanding of how moods, thoughts, and feelings shaped their experiences, they could see why their earlier efforts hadn't worked. Their focus on external fixes—like date nights, communication strategies, and attachment styles—was like trying to build a house starting with the roof instead of the foundation.

What truly transformed their relationship was the 'ground-up' approach: learning to understand and navigate their own inner world first. They saw that their connection didn't depend on doing more or getting everything right—it grew naturally when they stopped overcomplicating things and focused on the simple truths of the human experience.

This shift created a foundation of ease, resilience, and mutual understanding. No longer weighed down by techniques or strategies, they discovered a relationship that felt lighter, more authentic, and deeply connected. And from this grounded place, everything else began to fall into place.

Chapter 5

Busting relationship myths and misinformation

James and Sally were childhood sweethearts, together since high school. Now in their 60s, however, they seemed to be in constant conflict. James felt like Sally didn't appreciate him, she was always criticising him and putting him down. He worked long hours in a stressful job and had started to dread coming home.

Sally, on the other hand, felt like James never listened to her. She felt he prioritised his work and the children over her and was always seeing her in a negative light. She felt like she could never be herself around James, which over time had led to her shutting down around him. Sally felt sad and lonely in her marriage.

The couple had tried a number of different counselling options in the past, where they'd looked at their communication styles, personality types and their attachment and fighting styles. Things would improve for a little while, but they would soon end up back in the same place; angry, hurt, and distant from one another.

Sally believed their inability to communicate was their biggest issue, while James thought they couldn't move forward until *all* their problems were examined and resolved. But every time they

tried to talk about these issues, things would quickly escalate, resulting in them not speaking for days.

By the time James and Sally came to see me, they were in complete crisis. "Why can't we get along Fiona? Why do we find it so hard to have fun and connect? What is it that's missing?" Sally was at the point where they either work things out or they separate.

Many of us grow up believing this relationship advice to be true, but when we try to apply it to our relationships, often all it does is add to our overwhelm and feelings of disempowerment, making things so much harder.

This is because a lot of this advice is focused on external fixes, which is the fundamental flaw in building a relationship from the top down. Here are what I would call some of the most pervasive 'top down' relationship myths.

Myth #1 If only we could communicate better, our relationship would improve.

Fact. Communication itself is not the cause, it's merely a symptom of something else.

This is such a common refrain I hear from my clients. And on the surface, it seems logical. People who communicate well tend to get along with each other, so therefore focusing on communication would appear to be the answer.

However, good communication is not about applying a strategy or technique. There's something else at play here, which must be addressed first. A communication breakdown is not the main problem to solve, it's just a symptom of something else going on.

The simple truth is, we all communicate well when we feel good. When we feel good, communication is natural, easy, and effortless. So, when you understand how to address feeling good, communication tends to take care of itself.

Now, how much easier does that sound?

The bank of goodwill

So how do you address feeling good? It's all about goodwill.

Goodwill is a feeling of generosity, consideration, and friendliness towards another person. It's fundamental when it comes to relationships and communication.

Think of goodwill as a bit like compound interest for a relationship. With each small deposit, it grows two-fold. Like earning interest on your interest, goodwill creates goodwill, and the ripple effects are huge. If you focus on building and fostering a healthy balance of goodwill together first (which is a lot easier than you think), communication naturally takes care of itself.

A breakdown in communication usually coincides with a breakdown of goodwill. And so trying to improve or fix a 'communication issue' when there is an absence of goodwill is futile. Just think back to a moment of discord between you and your partner or someone you work with. Did you feel a desire to communicate warmly while you were feeling upset? I'd hazard a guess the answer is no. You might have even had the thought, *I never want to speak to that person again!*

A lack of goodwill is also the number one reason traditional relationship counselling often fails. This is because a counsellor will often bring a couple together who are usually in an insecure or low frame of mind, and therefore have little to no goodwill, and try to get them to communicate and sort their issues out.

It's a recipe for disaster. When two people are in an insecure frame of mind and have no goodwill toward each other, they can't access the level of understanding and compassion they need to genuinely problem solve. They tend to be suspicious of each other's intentions and get reactionary and defensive. They take things personally, they're unable to listen, and the blame game continues.

But when we come together from a space of goodwill, we give each other the benefit of the doubt or a free pass. We're more generous of mind and spirit, our sense of humour is intact, and we let things go. Trying to communicate and solve problems when we don't feel good makes no sense whatsoever, and only creates more of the same.

The moment that creating goodwill became more important to me than 'being right' and winning an argument, was the moment everything in my life became easier. These days, I am far more interested in feeling good than I ever was in proving a point.

Myth #2 Fixing the problems will fix the relationship.

Fact. Focusing on our problems only serves to lower our spirits, making issues harder to resolve.

Have you ever noticed that when you talk a lot about a problem you have, you don't feel so great? When we pore over the details of who said what and how that made us feel, it brings all the pain and hurt to vivid life in our minds, which in turn has us feeling discouraged and upset.

In this upset state of mind, we then attempt to find a solution, which now seems more impossible than ever. It feels like an enormous mountain to climb because all we can see is the problem in front of us. No wonder so many people think relationships are hard work!

The truth is, everything *looks* hard when we're in a discouraged and upset state of mind. We can't see clearly, and so our problems become magnified and distorted—and often something only starts to look like a problem when our thinking goes south, and we don't have clarity of mind.

When our thinking is healthy and our minds are clear, solutions and answers can seem obvious and easy, and we wonder why we couldn't see it before. That's because when we focus on the problem, all we see is the problem. Our concern simply creates more concern and can't provide us with the answers we're looking for.

After a few sessions together, I could see a significant change in James and Sally. Where once there had been tension and defensiveness, there was now a beautiful lightness between them. They were smiling at one another and giggling.

James shared a powerful insight, which had shifted everything for him. "All I could see was that we had all these problems to solve, and I was so fixated on them that I stopped seeing anything good between us."

He went on, "I've let go of fixing anything now, I'm no longer trying so hard. Things now feel effortless. I can see that Sally is just being Sally, there is no problem for me to fix. This has allowed me to be myself, to relax and let go. And the difference I've seen in Sally has been incredible, she's so much lighter and at ease around me."

With a light in her eye, Sally agreed, "I finally feel as though I can be myself. James is listening to me, everything is easier, and funnily enough, we're now talking and communicating quite naturally!"

As they were leaving, James added, "I always thought we had to fix our problems, and Sally thought we had to learn to communicate to move forward, but we haven't had to do any of that for us to reconnect and feel good around one another again. I wouldn't have believed it if I hadn't experienced this for myself."

Myth #3 We're too different to be compatible.

Fact. Compatibility is a feeling we experience and has little to do with how much we have in common.

The potential for compatibility is often just one new thought or perspective away. I've had many clients over the years tell me their relationships aren't working because they're just too different and are therefore incompatible. Yet when they first met, those same differences were a refreshing change.

The truth is, you don't need to have lots of things in common for a relationship to work. You don't need to have the same values or interests to be on the same page.

This is because compatibility is a feeling, not a checklist.

In other words, when we *feel* compatible with someone, we *are* compatible, regardless of how much we have in common or how different we are. It's really that simple.

I've had clients whose partners were their perfect match on paper. They shared the same interests, had similar personalities, they even dealt with conflict the same way. Yet they were stuck in the same painful cycle as a couple who were complete opposites.

This is because compatibility is more about how two people *feel* together, rather than what they do or don't do together. It all comes down to being in a good feeling and having goodwill toward one another. When you start to understand where that good feeling comes from, you have the potential to be compatible with anyone.

Compatible opposites

I've seen this play out with my own parents. My mum is an artist, a dreamy, creative visionary with a flair for the dramatic and different projects on the go. She also has no concept of time and is notoriously late for everything. Dad, on the other hand, is a practical numbers man and retired accountant. He prides himself on being punctual, is super focused and organised, and tends to see the world from a left-brain, logical perspective.

On the surface, they would not appear to have much in common, but it's never been an issue because they're so good at having fun together. They enjoy looking at life through the lens of the other, they see their differences as a point of interest rather than an incompatible deal breaker.

In a nutshell, they feel compatible, *and so they are.* They implicitly understand that the feeling they generate between them has nothing to do with their personalities or how compatible they are. They know the power of goodwill, and so together they've cultivated this warm feeling, prioritising time to ensure there is plenty of goodwill between them.

There are examples of this everywhere—people with very different personalities and interests, who either love one another and enjoy each other's company or work well together despite their differences. Our differences don't have to be the do-or-die crossroad in our relationships. It's possible to see them as a positive, and as an opportunity to grow and see something different.

Myth #4 You need good relationship role models to be good at relationships.

Fact. We're all born with the natural ability to be good at relationships, regardless of our role models. Love is who we are, it's our nature.

A lot of people live out of the misunderstanding that if they didn't have any positive relationship role models growing up, if the ones they had were toxic and destructive, then they won't be good at relationships themselves. And while a lack of good role models can create harmful habits in our relationships, it's not what holds us back from being good at them.

We all have an innate capability to experience wellbeing and connectedness to others. It's part of our human design. We come into this world in a state of wellbeing, it's our default state—and we return there whenever our mind is free of our problems, our past, and our future.

We do this naturally when our minds slow down. We return to 'home base' and a place of innate wellbeing where we all have access to love, connection, clarity and peace.

Our ability to access these qualities is not tied to whether we had good role models growing up. It's simply about knowing where to look. Understanding is the gift for all relationships and once you start to see this, you'll notice everything that's happened in your life previously begins to fall away and becomes less impactful—without lots of effort, technique, or application.

Myth #5 I'm not great at relationships because of things that have happened in the past.

Fact. Our past has far less bearing on what we're capable of than we think. What brings the past to life in the present moment is the 'thinking' we have about it.

Many of us believe our past determines our future. If you have this belief yourself, I want you to know it's simply not true. While it can feel vivid and real to us, it's not real in the present moment.

When we look at our past, we often develop a habit of thinking that it's a reflection of who we are today. But the past is never a reflection of who we can be now—this is an illusion created by our own thinking in the moment.

I often use the metaphor of a bruise to illustrate the impact of the past in our present lives. Imagine there's a bruise on your arm from a past injury. It's not that painful anymore but when you press it, it hurts and reminds you of the injury. Later you press it again to make sure it still hurts, and sure enough it still does.

We interact with our thinking about the past in much the same way. If we resist engaging with it, we stop bringing it into our present or our future. This opens up so many possibilities for our current relationships and our emotional freedom.

Myth #6 It takes two people to turn a relationship around.

Fact. One person is all it takes to create change.

It's a common belief that turning a relationship around requires equal effort from both people involved. This leads many to feel helpless, thinking that if their partner isn't willing to change, then what's the point. Or to stubbornly hold out till everyone is on the same page. But the truth is, lasting change can start with just one person.

Relationships act as mirrors, reflecting back to us what we project. When we change our own thoughts, feelings, and behaviours, we often see a ripple effect in our interactions and connections. This isn't about manipulation or forcing the other person to respond in a certain way. Instead, it's about aligning ourselves with what we want to experience in the relationship.

Here's where the power lies: by choosing to shift our perspective or embrace a new understanding, we can reshape the dynamic. When one person shifts, it naturally invites the other to respond to the new energy in a different way, sometimes even without consciously realising it. This is why a change in how we show up—the thinking we believe and engage with or our reactions and behaviours—can have a profound effect on our relationships.

Earlier in the book, I shared insights into my own relationship struggles prior to coming across this understanding. The truth is, I was able to turn my marriage around completely without my husband doing anything differently.

This was because I was the one who changed. I was the one who embraced a new understanding— and the gift of that understanding was shared. It had such a deep and profound impact on *us both* that today we're closer than ever, despite weathering some pretty big relationship storms together.

When we change within ourselves, that change is often powerfully reflected in the people and relationships around us. What's truly wonderful about this, is that one person alone can make an extraordinary difference to a situation.

Chapter 6

A simple truth - the power of a principle

In December 1903, the Wright brothers flew the first engine-powered aeroplane, and changed the history of aviation forever.

Through their scientific research, they had discovered something groundbreaking, the principles of flight: Lift, Thrust, Weight, and Drag.

Once they understood how these principles worked together, the Wright brothers knew no matter what the size or type of aircraft, if it could meet the principles of flight, it would fly. This discovery was revolutionary and paved the way for the design of every aeroplane we see today, from a tiny two-seater prop to a giant commercial airliner.

So for any pilot in training, it's not just about learning to operate the aircraft. They must also understand the principles of flight, because if anything goes wrong this is what they come back to.

This is the power of a principle.

Operating from a principle removes the guesswork and the complexity and makes everything easier. That is because principles are founded in truth. And a truth is only a truth if it applies to everybody all the time. Otherwise, it's simply an opinion.

An opinion is not a truth. An opinion is simply a thought captured in a moment and brought to life as fact.

There are a lot of opinions in the world that then become strategies or techniques. What's important to remember is that an opinion, strategy, or technique has a limited shelf life. It only applies to some people some of the time, not all people all the time.

Another great example of a truth is the force of gravity. Gravity works the exact same way for everybody and everything on the planet.

If I have a pen in my hand and I let it go, it will fall to the nearest surface in response to the force of gravity. If the King of England were to hold the same pen and let go, it would also fall to the nearest surface.

No matter who has the pen, once they let go, it will fall. We understand that gravity is a truth that applies the same way to everybody all the time.

So, let's keep looking in the direction of truth.

One of the most pervasive beliefs out there is that relationships are hard work, and we have to keep working hard in order to have a happy, successful one.

This is based on the premise that human beings are complex and complicated, and change is hard. So, we have to dig deep and do all this work to overcome the obstacles, like the endless differences between men and women, and figuring out our personality types and communication styles. Cue exhaustion.

Not surprisingly, this is all pretty daunting for our funny little human. It's why people are often so apprehensive about getting help. Because the mountain we're told we have to conquer to make our relationship work seems so high and impassable that it's easier to do nothing and quietly hope for the best.

But what if the opposite were true?

The power of a principle

What if there was a simple truth behind it all? That meant being in a happy, connected relationship could be easy and effortless for us all?

Well, I have some good news for you.

There are fundamental spiritual principles that all human beings live by. These principles are constants that exist whether we're aware of them or not. They govern the way we interact and move through the world.

Looking at life through the lens of a principle simplifies everything. It removes complexity and creates ease and flow.

The Oxford English Dictionary defines a principle as: "A fundamental truth or proposition that serves as the foundation for a system of belief or behaviour for a chain of reasoning."

In other words, a principle is a universal and fundamental truth or law that applies to everyone all the time, regardless of gender, religion, personality, or past experiences.

Why is this powerful?

A principle shows us that we're all connected.

It's the ultimate even playing field because the same rules apply to everyone. This is why a principle creates trust. A trust in something we can come back to again and again. But like most things in

life, the only way we can trust in something is by having a direct experience of it.

A principle lays a foundation of knowledge and understanding, which our funny little human can keep coming back to, regardless of our circumstances. This is incredibly powerful, no matter the application or situation.

It's a truth that allows for simplicity in everything we know and do, which is a soothing balm to the soul of our funny little human. Truth impacts us because it bypasses our noisy, intellectual mind and connects with our soul. It moves us. And our little human dearly wants to be moved by life, to feel fulfilled and nourished from the inside out.

Chapter 7

The principles of being human

For years, I had been searching for a deeper understanding and insight into human nature. While I learned so many fascinating things in my search, I knew there was something missing.

At that point, I'd been running my own private practice for a few years, working with individuals and couples, but I had a growing sense of disenchantment. I loved seeing my clients' progress, yet I felt they weren't fully discovering the magic within themselves.

Too often, they looked to me for the quick fix they were seeking, as though I held all the answers. I knew this approach wasn't empowering them in a lasting way, but at the time I couldn't see how to shift things.

The moment I came across these principles it all clicked. I knew this was it. I remember thinking to myself, "Whatever you've been looking for, you've just found it". I had a sense of peace and acceptance I'd not felt since I was a child.

I knew it would change everything. Not just in my own relationships and in the way I saw the world, but the way I approached my work as well. So, I reached out to all my clients, and invited them to a two-day event, completely free. I told them, "I have come across

something extraordinary, which I'm still learning about. But I want to share with you what I'm learning."

I was straight up with them about what this meant. "This is a profound shift in my understanding of human nature, and I can no longer continue teaching something based on techniques and strategies. If you'd like your money back, I'll understand and happily give you a full refund. But if you want to stick with me while I develop my understanding of this, I would be honoured."

To their credit, they all trusted me enough to come to the event and hear me out. At the end of the two days, every single one of my clients came to me and said, "I'm in."

My hope for you is that you will feel the same by the end of this book.

Let's dive in.

The Three Principles

There are three universal principles behind the psychological experience of every human being on the planet. These are:

1. The Principle of Universal or Divine Mind
2. The Principle of Consciousness
3. The Principle of Thought

These principles are constants, they're always present whether we're aware of them or not. Our funny little human is governed by these universal forces every minute of every day.

Sydney Banks first introduced the Principles to the world in the early 1970s, as a way of understanding the human experience. An ordinary man, who was working as a welder at the time, Banks had what he described as an experience of profound spiritual enlightenment.

It was an insight into our true nature as human beings, and it revealed a deeper truth about how life works, and who and what we are. And it completely changed his life. He went on to become a world-renowned philosopher, educator, and author.

In his book *The Missing Link: Reflections on Philosophy and Spirit*, Banks writes, "Mind, Consciousness, and Thought are spiritual gifts that enable us to see creation and guide us through life."

Let's take a look at each one.

The Principle of Universal Mind

Divine or Universal Mind is the higher intelligence behind all life, it is the energy of all things. It powers our thoughts and our beating heart, the moon, the sun, the Universe, and everything in between.

Mind is the infinite space from which our personal thought and consciousness, our very existence, comes from. It's the source of creation and life itself that religions speak of and has many names in many different cultures.

Universal Mind is ever present, ever constant, and unchangeable. It ensures that life continues, that winter follows autumn, and night follows day.

By comparison, our own personal mind is constantly changing and busy. It's when we manage to slow down the chatter of our mind that moments of seemingly divine inspiration or intuition occur.

There's a reason why our best ideas come when we're in the shower, on holiday, or taking a walk. Why? Because our personal mind is quieter in those moments, allowing space for inspiration, insight, and fresh ideas to flow.

Albert Einstein summed this up well when he said, "Imagination is more important than knowledge. Knowledge is limited. Imagination encircles the world."[1]

This connection to a deeper wisdom comes from the Universal Mind, to which we are all connected. This is how true transformational change takes place within a human being, through moments of profound insight and realisation.

As Banks says, "There is one Universal Mind, common to all, and wherever you are, it is always with you, always."[2]

The Principle of Consciousness

Divine Consciousness is the universal awareness that connects all of us. It's an innate intelligence that transcends the individual mind and allows us to experience life on a deeper, more insightful level.

Consciousness is the foundation of our being, giving rise to the thoughts, feelings, and perceptions that shape our reality. Through this, we access a profound sense of clarity, wisdom, and understanding, reflecting the interconnected nature of all things. Consciousness is our awareness of life.

It gives us our innate capacity to experience and understand life as a conscious, sentient being. It helps us interpret the kind of experience we're having, whether it's good or bad. As Banks says, "Consciousness is the gift of awareness."[3]

Without Consciousness, we wouldn't be able to make sense of our thinking. It would simply be a stream of unintelligible thoughts

---

[1] Albert Einstein, *What Life Means to Einstein: An Interview by George Sylvester Viereck* (The Saturday Evening Post, 1929).

[2] Sydney Banks, *The Missing Link: Reflections on Philosophy and Spirit* (Lone Pine Publishing, 1998).

[3] Sydney Banks, *The Missing Link: Reflections on Philosophy and Spirit* (Lone Pine Publishing, 1998).

passing unnoticed through our minds. Consciousness is the beam of light and understanding that allows us to make sense of it all.

Our own personal perception of consciousness may change, rising and falling with our thoughts and moods. We cycle through high and low levels of consciousness all the time. But Consciousness as a spiritual principle is a constant, pure, and unwavering awareness. It's unaffected by whatever our personal perception might be in the moment.

The Principle of Thought

Divine Thought is the ultimate creative power.

It enables us to take the pure creative energy of Universal Mind, and channel it into ideas and images and feelings. Thought is how we create our own individual experience of reality. It's our ability to think.

Like our personal mind and our perception of consciousness, our own personal thinking is constantly changing. But the Principle of Thought is much bigger than the stream of thoughts constantly passing through our minds. It's a formless energy brought to life by the power of Consciousness.

Every feeling we experience comes from a thought we have had. We think something, which in turn makes us feel something in response. And every time our thoughts change, the feeling we have changes accordingly. This means our experience of life always comes from within, created from our own minds.

As Banks says, "Thought is not reality, yet it is through thought that our realities are created."[4]

---

[4] Sydney Banks, *The Missing Link: Reflections on Philosophy and Spirit* (Lone Pine Publishing, 1998).

When Sydney had the realisation that all his insecurity and anxiety was just a temporary thought creation, he said it "felt like a bomb went off in my head and a lifetime of insecurity lifted from my shoulders."[5]

He knew that every single one of us had the capacity to wake up to the creative power of Thought.

The Principles in action

So, what does all this mean for our funny little human?

Over time, our human has learned to live in what looks like a world of external experiences. Something happens 'out there' in the world, and we believe we feel something in response to that.

The direction of the process is the key. Even though it looks like the cause of our feelings are these external circumstances, this outside thing that's happening around us, the true cause of our feelings in any given moment is our thinking. It comes from *inside* us. Not outside. With no exception.

Life is in fact an 'inside out' experience, generated via the gift of Thought, Mind and Consciousness, in any given moment of now.

That's a mouthful, I know. Let's take a moment to allow this to sink in.

As you let this idea settle, consider the possibility that every feeling you've ever had was born within you—not from the world around you, but from the thoughts flowing through you in each moment.

Your thinking and you

The most important aspect of the relationship you have with you is the relationship you have with your own thinking.

---

[5] Sydney Banks, *The Enlightened Gardener* (Lone Pine Publishing, 2001).

This is because your own thinking is what lies between you and everything in your life. I often explain to my clients and students, "You're never in a direct relationship with another person. Between you and every relationship you have, is *your thinking about that person*. When your thinking changes, so does your relationship with that person."

This is why we all have the power to make a profound difference in a relationship, no matter what the situation is.

Paul's story

Recently, I was on a live call with the students from my Relatable program. These calls are always very special; there's a magic we create together that connects us, and we look forward to them each week.

During this call, one of my students was talking about difficulties with his engraving business. Paul felt his clients were hard work, there wasn't much money in it, and he just wanted to sell and get rid of the business.

Since joining Relatable, Paul had experienced an enormous shift in understanding. He could see that how he showed up to his life and the people around him mattered, and how much the quality of his thinking impacted this. Recently he'd decided to change his attitude toward his business. No matter what a client said or did, he intended to be kind, friendly, patient, and more appreciative of them.

"I noticed an immediate change in how I experienced my business," Paul said. "I started looking forward to going into work, I was having conversations with clients I hadn't had before, I made time for people. Clients began sending me referrals, and the business started making more money. I even began dressing differently. My clients noticed and one of them remarked, 'Wow Paul you look

great, I didn't realise what a handsome guy you are, you should wear those colours more often'."

Paul then went on to share a story about an elderly client of his called Bob, who never spent much money and always wanted a chat—something Paul never had time for previously.

One day, Bob came into the shop and Paul, with his newfound awareness, pulled up a chair and offered him a cup of tea. "I really enjoyed speaking with him," Paul said. "He shared so many interesting stories about our area. He's a really lovely guy."

A few weeks later, Bob came back in to the shop. Paul noticed that he didn't seem himself and asked if everything was okay. Bob admitted that his wife had recently passed away and he was really missing her. Her ashes were in a box on his kitchen table, but he didn't know what to do with them.

Struck by this, Paul said, "How about I make a nice plaque for your wife's ashes?" Bob's lit up face was all he needed in response. Paul said the job only took about half an hour of his time and a few dollars in materials. When Bob returned a few days later, Paul showed him the plaque and they put it on the box which contained his wife's ashes.

With tears streaming down his face, Bob came around the workbench and wrapped his arms around Paul in a tight hug. Paul was deeply moved by the impact this small gesture had had on another human being, "I can't explain the gift it gave me," he said.

After that, Bob's friends at various clubs all started coming into the shop, on Bob's glowing recommendation. And they all brought their club trophies to be engraved. "I can't tell you how good this feels," Paul marvelled. "I could never go back to showing up the way I was. Even our family cat wants to sit on my lap. The cat has never wanted anything to do with me the entire 12 years we've owned it!"

Your relationship with your thinking

The more we take our own thinking personally, and the more we believe every single thought we have, the more we are at the mercy of what we think.

Our own thinking is the greatest con artist on earth, the most convincing costume at the fancy dress party. Thoughts can appear vivid and real in our minds, yet the truth is, they're often a highly unreliable source of information.

This is because our thoughts are not facts. Just because we think something, doesn't make it real or true. And just because we might have had the same thoughts about something for years and years has no bearing on its validity or truth.

By nature, we are thinkers. Our funny little humans all live in a world of thought. We're thinking, thinking, thinking all the time. There is nothing we experience from birth to death, from beginning to end, that isn't brought to life via the power of Thought.

But we are not what we think.

The power and nature of Thought, and the content of what we think are two very different things. This is an important distinction to make, as our little human tends to get duped by its own thinking and innocently misuses the power of Thought against itself.

High mood and low mood thinking

The nature of Thought is unchanging and unchangeable, it undulates through us and as it does so, it moves up and down. Which means the quality of our thinking moves up and down with it.

There are times where the quality of our thinking is of a higher level, and this lifts our mood. We can call this high mood thinking.

High mood thinking feels lighter. It's generally more philosophical, understanding, and compassionate. It feels loving, curious, and playful.

There are also moments where the quality of our thinking is of a lower level, and this lowers our mood. We can call this low mood thinking.

Low mood thinking tends to be heavier in nature and is more ego and self-focused. With low mood thinking, our human is prone to thoughts of self-righteousness, anxiousness, guilt, blame, unfairness, and depression. It has less patience, compassion, and understanding.

For example, let's say you walk in the door from work, and your partner barely looks at you or says hello. Now with a higher level of awareness, you might look at your partner and your compassionate, high mood thinking might be, *Oh they look really tired. I know they had that big presentation at work today, I wonder how it went? I might see if they'd like a hot bath, and I'll take care of dinner tonight.*

There is so much understanding and kindness in the quality of that thinking and this creates a feeling of patience, love, and connection.

In contrast, from a lower level of awareness, your low mood thinking might be, *What's the matter with them now? I really can't deal with their moodiness today. I've been at work all day too. Is it too much to ask for a simple hello? If they aren't going to bother saying something nice, then I'm not going to either.*

The situation is the same but the quality of your thinking, be it high or low mood, has a major impact on how you experience it. Without an understanding of the Principle of Thought, a human with low mood thinking will naturally think the reason they're feeling this way is because of their partner.

That human will then make that mean something about the other person or the state of their relationship. More low mood thinking follows and things often quickly go downhill from there.

This is not to say that low mood thinking is wrong or bad. We all have low mood thinking from time to time, it's a natural and normal part of the human experience. It's not something we have to 'work on', the nature of something is unchangeable, after all.

But it's important to understand the nature of low mood thinking and how it can distort the lens through which we view the world.

When we realise that these thoughts aren't a true reflection of reality, and that they're simply a temporary state, we can take them less seriously. The more deeply we understand this, the less frightened we become of our experience of life.

Unlimited potential

Most traditional therapy and personal development has us focus on the content of our thinking. Instead, what I am pointing to here is not the content of our thinking, but *what powers it.*

When I talk about the Principle of Thought, I am not referring to the endless thoughts that constantly flow through your mind. That is your own *personal* thinking.

The Principle of Thought that Sydney Banks identified is much bigger than this. It allows for the creation of all reality, it's an energy field of unlimited potential from which everything is perceived.

We're all connected to this field, every single one of us, without exception.

It is through this connection that we get to paint pictures in our mind, to create our reality in any given moment. We are making it all up as we go along. All of it.

As Banks says, "Your thoughts are like the artist's brush. They create a personal picture of the reality you live in."[6]

The power lies not in the specific thoughts you have, but in the fact that you can think in the first place. That ability is far more powerful than any single thought or idea you entertain.

Our thinking is always changing

Life isn't something that just happens *to* us; it unfolds *through us.*

Our thoughts are a stream of consciousness flowing through us automatically all day long. We're all subject to and at the mercy of this constant stream (we can't exactly walk into a 'thought store' and choose only the thoughts we want!).

Our thoughts are also unreliable, because they're a reflection only of our state of mind at any given moment, not of what's true out there in the world.

And so the content of our thinking is always changing. Fresh thoughts, old thoughts, judgemental thoughts, resentful thoughts, anxious thoughts, loving thoughts, joyful thoughts. This is why trying to rein in and control our thinking, to only think 'positive thoughts', is an exercise in futility.

Instead of trying to change the content of our thinking, wouldn't it be easier to recognise that our funny little human is simply doing the best it can based on the quality of thinking it has in any given moment?

Instead of struggling against the tide of its own thinking, wouldn't it be easier for our human to float downstream and wait for a healthier, more helpful thought to come along?

---

[6] Sydney Banks, *The Missing Link: Reflections on Philosophy and Spirit* (Lone Pine Publishing, 1998).

If we understand that it's normal to have high mood and low mood thinking, that we don't choose our thoughts and these thoughts have no bearing on who we are, it becomes easier to recognise we are just thinking in the moment, and that our thinking might not be so trustworthy right now.

Low mood thinking tends to exaggerate the negative stuff. The nature of low mood thinking has us feeling more worried and concerned, it highlights our fears and concerns, and makes problems look bigger than they are. Low mood thinking has us looking at issues and differences through a magnifying glass, creating a frightening illusion for our poor little human.

2025 — Jan 12

This is why the advice to 'sleep on it' is so effective. When we feel stuck or worried, waiting until the next day to make a decision allows time for Thought to do what it does best—bring us an insight or fresh thinking. And because fresh thinking comes from Universal Mind, the higher intelligence behind life that flows through us all, this thinking is always going to be of a higher, more loving quality.

The wisdom of waiting for clearer thinking

Now if my little human understands all this—that this is the way Thought itself works and this is the way its own personal mind works—what is it likely to do differently when low mood thinking sets in?

Instead of blurting out whatever is on its mind and saying something hurtful or defensive, instead of raising its voice and getting angry at someone it cares about, my little human will have the life-changing capacity in any given moment to recognise that it simply has low mood thinking.

My human understands that low mood thinking can't be trusted because it exaggerates worry and concern, and reduces emotional intelligence. Something that is true for all humans.

Armed with this powerful understanding and awareness, my human is now more likely to wait until that low mood thinking has passed. It's more likely to wait until its mind has cleared and it has access to more reliable thinking. From there, with fresh thinking, it can handle or approach a situation completely differently. With a completely different outcome.

Lifting the emotional fog

With low mood thinking our human operates in an emotional fog with no real clarity. It can't listen effectively because its mind is full of everything that's wrong. It's more likely to take things personally, it's more likely to pick a fight, have a critical tone, or be in a heightened state of dissatisfaction.

 From this state of mind, our human gathers evidence by going back into the past to prove its point, cataloguing every other time this situation has happened. It gets obstinate, doubles down and projects its fears, worries and opinions onto the people around it, wreaking havoc.

But with high mood thinking, the fog lifts, and our innocent human can see beyond its own insecurities. The need to defend, judge or hide falls away. From there a more loving, compassionate, and curious minded human emerges. One that feels better, calmer, and emotionally intelligent.

It can even find some of the extremes of its earlier low mood thinking funny! It can be playful with its insecurities because it understands these are nothing more than illusionary thoughts that only look real when low mood thinking sets in.

Knowing that we're all governed by the Principle of Thought, that we all have low mood thinking that looks deceptively real, and we all say and do things we don't mean when that low mood thinking takes hold, our human can see how similar we all are, how normal it is for this to happen, and that there is nothing broken and nothing to fix.

The ripple effect begins

At this point, the opportunity to see our own psychological innocence in all this emerges. This allows us to start letting ourselves off the hook when we get hoodwinked by our own thinking. And once we can see this for ourselves, we can see this for every other human too.

We feel more confident in our ability to handle difficult situations and emotions with ease. This means we relax, our mind slows down, and our emotional and mental bandwidth increases. All without having to do any hard work on ourselves, without having to manage, change or overcome our thinking.

Simply through understanding the Principle of Thought.

When we know that we're just one thought away from a totally different experience, imagine the impact on our quality of life and our relationships. We stop taking things so personally, we stop resisting our experience, and we allow our low mood thinking to pass without getting frightened or stuck.

The impact is extraordinary.

Our human is now less critical of itself and others, and less likely to attack and judge. It's more forgiving, understanding, compassionate and emotionally intelligent. This is the true potential for everyone.

Because of the power of the Three Principles of Divine Mind, Divine Consciousness and Divine Thought, every funny little human has the potential to have any experience around anything. A potential that's only limited by how much we believe our own personal thinking.

Chapter 8

Our psychological immune system

David was a high achiever, who prided himself on being in control and on top of it all. But the increasing effort it took for him to manage everything in his life—problems at work, home and especially his relationship with his partner Seb—were wearing him down.

A tenacious problem-solver, David's mind was always in overdrive, focused on preventing any potential problems and issues or nipping them in the bud quickly. He was always looking for the problem, and while this skill was helpful at work, it was paralysing his relationship.

David would analyse Seb's every word and action, which had Seb feeling self-conscious and guarded. David couldn't understand why, with all his best efforts and hyper-vigilance, he and Seb were clashing more than ever.

It was clear how overwhelmed, emotionally drained, and tightly wound David was from bearing this immense mental load. I knew telling him to let go would not be helpful in that state. He was too deeply wired to fix everything; he believed it was all on him. So, I chose a different approach.

I asked David if he'd ever thought about what a self-sufficient system the human body was. How it handles so many complex internal processes on its own, like breathing, digesting, and healing. Surprised, he considered this for a moment. "I've never thought about it like that before but you're right. It's pretty cool actually when you think about it."

I followed this up with a second question. "What if your mind could do the same thing?"

The innate intelligence of our psychology

When it comes to our physical body, there's not much we're in charge of. Our cells and organs all function without our say so. We don't have to remember to keep our heart beating or our blood pumping. We don't have to oversee our adrenal or hormonal systems.

In fact, we have all these vital physiological processes that function seamlessly by themselves. Of course, there are things we have to do to support our physical body—we need to stay hydrated, eat nutritious food and get enough rest—but our entire system is automated. It requires no manual input from us because the intelligence behind every single cell in our body is always running the show.

We have this extraordinary, self-protecting mechanism built-in called our immune system. And we trust in this, don't we? We know, for the most part, if we feel unwell the best thing we can do is rest and allow our immune system to do its thing—bring us back to physical health.

So, consider this for a moment. Why would we be so perfectly designed with a physical system that's totally automated, but a psychological system that's on manual override?

It doesn't make sense, does it?

Our psychological immune system

Might there be a possibility that the divine intelligence that designed our amazingly automated human form, with an immune system that protects and restores our physical health, might also have devised a way to restore our psychological health? That just like our physical immune system, we might also have a psychological immune system?

That makes more sense, right?

Yet because we believe our psychological system is entirely on manual override, we resist it, we fight against it. We think it's on us to manage it and fix it.

In other words, our confused little human keeps getting in the way and unwittingly making life much harder for itself and its relationships.

The truth is, we all have a remarkable psychological immune system that is beautifully, magnificently, and lovingly designed to not only take us back to wellbeing, but to take us from one experience to another with no effort required on our behalf.

Just like the cells within our bodies, there's an intelligence and wisdom within us all that knows exactly what it's doing. And via the gift of fresh thinking and awareness that is our birthright, we go back to wellbeing automatically.

This is the nature of the human experience, this is the nature of Thought, and this is the nature of Consciousness.

A weight lifted

At first, this idea was unthinkable to David. He was so used to relying on his intellect to manage everything, and his problem-solving skills and determination to fix and make things right.

Intrigued but sceptical, he agreed to test this theory out. Rather than diving into a mental analysis whenever he felt triggered, or rushing to fix someone else's problem, he would try to pause. He'd

see if his mind could settle naturally on its own and let things play out.

An opportunity soon presented itself. His partner Seb came home from work, upset about being overlooked for a promotion he'd been working towards. David felt his familiar urge to rush in and fix the situation. He was about to interrupt Seb with suggestions and solutions, but remembering our conversation, decided to sit with his feelings instead.

To his surprise, David felt his mind begin to quiet. The urgency to jump in and make Seb feel better slowly eased and understanding showed up in its place. He listened while Seb talked, held space for his upset and felt strangely calm and closer to him than he had in a long time.

By giving himself the space to let his mind settle on its own, David could see the situation with so much more clarity. He wasn't responsible for fixing Seb's emotions—or even his own. This insight lifted a weight from his shoulders he hadn't even realised he was carrying, allowing him to handle the situation completely differently.

Instead of reacting with urgency, he responded with compassion. In that moment, David experienced the profound shift of stepping back and trusting his psychological immune system to do its job. He didn't need to manually manage his emotions or mental state— his mind had the capacity to return to balance all on its own. Seb noticed the change in him immediately.

A few days later, Seb shared the newfound openness he felt with him, "It feels like we're finally on the same team again." This struck David deeply. In letting go of the need to fix everything—for Seb or himself—and simply allowing his mind to settle, David created space for genuine connection to naturally re-emerge in their relationship.

The gift of awareness

Consciousness is the gift of awareness that enables us to look within ourselves and have an awareness of the space we're coming from and what we are creating.

Without this precious gift, we would be flying blind. It would be like going to the movies and watching the screen with no lights or sound. Think of Thought as the movie on the big screen, and Consciousness as the beam of light through the projector that brings the movie to life.

How is this important when it comes to love and relationships?

Consciousness allows us to see the level of thinking we have; it highlights the state of mind we're in. For example, let's imagine I'm in a bad mood, and I feel like my kids are being lazy and disrespectful because they haven't done what I asked them to do.

If I have no awareness or understanding of where my experience is coming from, then I'll continue to have the same thinking about my children, that they don't listen, that they're being lazy and disrespectful. I will gather all the evidence to confirm this is true, and address the issue with that same level of thinking.

How effective do you think that will be?

I will create upset, because I'm in an upset state of mind. Instead of listening, my kids will go straight into defence mode and argue with my mood, and the entire cycle goes around and around.

There's always another way

But what if I could see this feeling as a function of my own mind and not necessarily something my kids are creating?

What if I could understand the nature of Thought, that I am a thinker, and I simply have thinking I can't trust right now?

I'm going to have the capacity and the bandwidth to handle the situation completely differently.

Now I can recognise that I'm in low mood thinking. Divine Consciousness enables me to do this. I pause, I look within, and I realise that my state of mind is unreliable. I know I need to wait for fresh thinking. Because I can see this, I'm able to hold off until I feel calmer and my mind clears, just as it's designed to do.

I get access to fresh thinking, and with that comes the realisation that I have a thinking problem, rather than an 'out there' problem. I let go, I relax, and instead of yelling, I use humour to connect with my kids. I get curious, and gently chide, "Hey, is there any reason you haven't taken the bins out yet?"

"Whoops sorry Mum, I forgot. I'll do it now."

We now have potential for a completely different type of conversation— thanks to my understanding of where my experience is coming from and my awareness of my state of mind. Nothing else has changed.

The capacity to know when we're emotionally intelligent (and when we're not), to understand our low and high mood thinking, and to see it all as impersonally as we do the weather, this is the gift that Divine Consciousness brings to our lives and our relationships.

Consciousness is like a highlighter for our thinking, it can highlight the good stuff (and the not so good stuff).

'The how' line

When we're looking outward and we're focused on our memories of the past, or our behaviour, personality or the content of our thinking, our awareness shrinks, and our minds become smaller. We begin to feel isolated and disconnected from the whole, like we're the only ones having this issue.

I call this point 'the how' line.

How can I change this? How do I control this? How am I going to fix this? How do I overcome this? How can I be okay with this?

And as we cycle around 'the how' we begin to overthink and ruminate, and we go back in the past. We worry about the future, our imagination runs wild, and we get frightened. Our personal thinking mind starts racing and as a result we become reactionary. We no longer have the mental and emotional bandwidth we need to handle life.

This low mood state of mind is being brought to life via the Principle of Consciousness. Consciousness is neutral, just like the Principle of Thought, it's our personal thinking that adds the flavour.

When my consciousness is low, I'm fixated on 'the how' and life feels a lot more personal and intense. In this state, it's easy to get caught up in my own thoughts and take them as absolute truth.

But when my consciousness is higher, I gain the clarity to see where my experience truly comes from. I can recognise that it's all just Thought, flowing through me, moment by moment. I'm able to see the illusory nature of my experience and trust in the natural flow of Thought.

This shift allows me to see things anew, with a fresh perspective that opens up possibilities I couldn't see before.

In this elevated state, my thinking becomes more compassionate, neutral, loving, and curious. I can respond to life with a clearer mind, prepared to handle whatever arises. With this awareness, I understand when I'm showing up from a place that generates love, or when I'm showing up from a place that generates upset.

Neither state is inherently right or wrong. The real gift is in seeing my experience as it is, allowing me to adjust accordingly and meet life from a place of choice and clarity.

Riders of the storm

Our human experience is very similar to the weather.

The nature of the weather is neutral, impersonal, and unchanging. The weather itself may change—seasons change throughout the year, and the daily temperature and conditions may change throughout the day—but the nature of the weather does not.

There may be times we don't enjoy the weather, but we all accept it's something we can't control. We know the weather isn't personal and it can change unexpectedly, because that's what the weather does.

The nature of it is far bigger than us, and we accept that the nature of something is unchangeable. It's not something we have any control over. So, when the weather does turn suddenly, we may not be happy about it, but we adjust to it. It's the difference between saying, *Oh it's raining, I better grab an umbrella* and *I don't want it to rain, I need to make it stop!*

One understands the nature of the weather and works with it. The other fights against something that's futile to resist once you know how it works.

I used to dread the coming of winter, I was what you'd call 'weather affected'. Before we even got to the end of summer, I'd be counting the days until spring. I'd watch the days gradually shorten and grow darker, fretting about how I was going to deal with the winter cold.

I fantasised about moving north to a warmer climate. I'd look at the leaves changing colour on the trees, and instead of enjoying the beauty of nature as the season turned, all I could see was gloomy evidence of the impending winter. It would really affect me, and I'd get quite low about it.

I decided I just wasn't a 'winter person' (whatever that means) and because I'd had this thinking for years, I assumed it must be true. I made it mean all sorts of things about my relationship with winter.

It was only after I began to understand the Principles that I started to see this differently. It wasn't about whether or not I was a 'winter person' or how I felt about cold weather. I simply had so much habitual negative thinking about winter that I saw my thinking as fact. And because of this I was living in that reality—a reality I had created.

I could now see that my fear and dread of winter was my own creation. I wasn't 'weather affected', I didn't have to move thousands of miles away from family and friends to escape it. I just needed to see where and how my experience was being created, moment by moment.

Let me tell you, this was *freeing*.

I stopped dreading winter. I no longer counted the days until spring. In fact, I can honestly say I don't think much about winter at all anymore. I enjoy being cosy and warm around a fire while the wind howls outside. It's a reminder of how lucky I am to be warm and safe. I even like the earlier nights and see them as an opportunity to spend more time with my family, snuggling and relaxing. Rugging up to go outside in the crisp winter air is something I now relish.

It's been so interesting to see my entire experience of the weather change, as the relationship with my thinking around winter changed. To know that I am only ever a thought away from having a different experience of anything has been one of the greatest gifts to ever come into my life.

Chapter 9

The link between thought and feeling

A few years ago, I was in the U.S. working with George and Linda Pransky, mentors of mine at the time. George and I were sitting together in their living room, and I was sharing some frustration I was feeling with one of my teenagers at home.

George listened for a moment, then he smiled and in his deep drawl, said "You know Fiona, feelings are such an unreliable source of information."

I couldn't believe what I was hearing. I'd spent my whole life relying on my feelings to help me navigate through life. Isn't that what they were for? To be told they were not a reliable source of information turned everything I thought I knew on its head.

"If I can't rely on my feelings, what am I supposed to do? How do I..?" I couldn't even finish the sentence; I was so bewildered. He chuckled, "It's not that you can't rely on them, you just need to understand what they're actually telling you". The conversation that followed completely changed how I handled my emotions, my feelings, and my thinking from that moment forward.

It gave me a whole new understanding and insight into my relationship with my own intense feelings and emotions. Emotions that had me convinced that my ingrained habitual thinking was true. This thinking could do an emotional takeover of my poor little human in a split second, without me even realising it.

If you've ever felt at the mercy of your emotions, whether you're someone who explodes, shuts down or somewhere in between, I hope what I'm about to share with you is as powerful for your human as it was for mine.

We can transcend our experience

We live in the feeling of our thinking. We do not live in the feeling of anything else. In other words, life is experienced from the inside out. This is what we learn as we bring the Three Principles into our awareness.

Sydney Banks described this moment of awareness like this:

"My whole world just exploded in front of me. It was so simple that it just broke me through into separate realities, and it was devastatingly beautiful that all my problems dropped away. They all started flashing past me as fantasies because I started to realise that insecurity was thought…

"All of a sudden to find out that it's all thought, just thought manifesting into a feeling. The realisation was so beautiful that I never slept for three days and three nights."[7]

It was such a relief for me to know that I was not at the mercy of things external to me, and I didn't need the world or a person to change for me to have a different experience. Knowing that we have

---

[7] Sydney Banks, *The Best of Two Worlds - audio recording* (Lone Pine Publishing, date unknown).

this inbuilt capacity to transcend our experience was incredibly liberating.

In his memoir, *Man's Search for Meaning*, Viktor Frankl recounts his lived experience of the horror of Auschwitz and other concentration camps during the Holocaust. Frankl shares how he discovered at times a deeper meaning and spiritual freedom that took him away from the misery and horror he was experiencing.

"Everything can be taken from a man but one thing: the last of human freedoms—to choose one's attitude in any given set of circumstances, to choose one's own way. In the final analysis, it becomes clear that the sort of person the prisoner became was the result of an inner decision and not the result of camp influences alone."[8]

Attitude + gratitude!

We have all seen or heard of stories where human beings, after enduring great suffering and distress, have found this capacity within themselves to forgive and let go of the hurt and pain caused to them by another.

There's always another way

A powerful example of this that will stay with me forever, is the story of the Abdallah family in Sydney, Australia. They lost three of their young children and a young cousin in a terrible accident caused by a driver under the influence of drugs and alcohol.

What made it even more tragic was it was the first time the children were allowed to walk by themselves to the corner store to get ice cream. On their way there, a man lost control of his car and struck the group of children, killing four of them instantly.

It was a deeply distressing story that reverberated around the world. How could anyone get through a loss so unimaginable?

---

[8] Victor Frankl, *Man's Search for Meaning* (Beacon Press, 2006).

And yet what was even more extraordinary, was the attitude of the children's parents.

Shortly after the tragedy, Danny and Leila Abdallah made a statement saying they did not want the memory of their children to be tainted by ugliness, revenge, and bitterness. Despite their immense pain and grief, they said they had forgiven the driver.

I remember at the time thinking what an incredible, powerful example they were for millions of people, showing that even in the face of something so horrific, there was always another way. We are not locked into an experience. We always have choice and agency for ourselves.

The true potential of any human being is the innate capacity we all possess to have any experience around anything.

The true role our feelings play

We know now that the nature of Thought is neutral and transient, it moves through us on its own. And we know that the nature of something is unchangeable.

We also know that our personal thinking is highly unreliable, that we have high mood and low mood thinking, or healthy and unhealthy thinking, which is brought to life via the gift of Consciousness.

We understand that our personal thinking can create illusionary mirages in our mind, and that most of what we think can be taken with a grain of salt. We know that our thinking at times is more egoic, and at other times more philosophical.

The question now is, how does our poor human, who gets so easily distracted and caught up in its thinking, navigate its way through all these untrustworthy, deceptive, and unpredictable streams of thought?

This is where the true role our feelings play takes centre stage.

The link between thought and feeling

If we live in the feeling of our thinking, then our feelings a reliable indicator of whether our personal thinking is hea unhealthy. It's not about whether we believe our thinking is or not, nor whether our feelings are calm or upset. Instead, it's what those feelings tell us about our current state of mind.

Think of it like the weather; it's not so much about the actual temperature, but what the temperature tells us. If it's 10 degrees Celsius, for example, I know it's cold, so I'll grab a coat. Similarly, our feelings act as a gauge, signalling whether our state of mind is clear or clouded.

Our feelings, like a weather forecast, don't reveal the details of what's going on outside. They simply tell us whether the state we're in calls for attention or adjustment. They're always pointing us back to our own internal weather patterns, giving us insight into our present state of mind.

Choosing to pause

Imagine that you're having low mood thinking, and you start thinking about your partner; how different you are, how many times you've argued recently, and how unsupported you feel. As you think about all this, you start feeling angry and resentful in response. You keep following this train of thought and get so upset that you decide you need to act on it.

So you tell your partner how unhappy you are, that you have nothing in common and you're simply not compatible. You project all these upset feelings onto your partner. With each word, you become more upset, and because you innocently believe that your feelings are an indicator of truth, you see your upset as confirmation you're right.

As your upset feelings grow in intensity, it feels even more urgent to let loose and tell your partner everything you're feeling, and what you don't like about them. This erupts into a big fight, your partner shuts down and you go to bed feeling exhausted, upset, and drained.

However, as your mind rests, your personal thinking begins to quiet down. Fresh thoughts and insights start to surface, and by morning, you realise you were just feeling tired and stressed. Regret sets in as you remember the things you said in the heat of the moment—things you didn't really mean, and you now wish you could take back.

So what has changed? Only your level of awareness and the shift in your thinking. But the damage has been done; your partner feels hurt and upset, and the goodwill between you has taken a serious hit.

Imagine how differently this might play out if you understood the Principle of Thought in that moment. Recognising that you were simply experiencing low mood thinking, you could have chosen to pause and let your mind settle before reacting. By waiting, you'd have given yourself the chance to respond from a clearer state of mind.

All the emotional upset, pain, and disconnection could have been avoided entirely. It's these kinds of moments that destabilise relationships, leaving both partners feeling like they're walking on eggshells, uncertain why things have become so difficult.

The reality our thoughts create

Here's another scenario.

Let's say you're driving home from work. You've had a pretty good day, and you're looking forward to getting home. You turn into the street where you live, and a thought about your partner pops into your head:

The link between thought and feeling

I wonder what kind of mood they're in? They were really grumpy last night. I hope they don't want to talk about anything too intense, I just want to relax, I don't need the drama.

Immediately in response, you start to feel tense and your stomach clenches. You pull into the driveway. Another thought, *How come I only feel like this when I'm coming home? I don't feel like this when I'm at work, I only feel like this around them.*

Your sense of disquiet grows, you walk inside, now wary and defensive. Your partner senses this and without understanding why, tenses up in return. Feeling their tension, you quickly walk down the hall to avoid any conflict, saying you're going to take a shower.

By now, your partner is feeling hurt and confused that you haven't said hello. Their little human starts innocently having low mood thinking. They begin to feel unappreciated, and they think of all the times you haven't noticed the things they've done to make your life better. They begin to think about how much happier they were feeling before you walked in the door, and they begin to wonder if they would be happier on their own.

This is how quickly our low mood thinking can escalate.

Meanwhile, you're thinking about how well your day was going until you came home, and that you actually feel pretty good when you're not around your partner. You also start to wonder if the relationship is right for you.

For many people, this can become a continuous cycle of reacting and fault-finding. They'll start spending less and less time together, living out of their low mood thinking and draining their goodwill, until they no longer feel good around one another, and one or both walks away from the relationship.

Now let's rewind and go back to that drive home from work, except this time you have an understanding of the Principles.

This time, you notice where your mind is going and before you get enrolled in that thinking, you check in on the feeling you're in. You understand that how your feeling is an indicator of how healthy or unhealthy your thinking is, and right now your feeling has nose-dived. You realise it has nothing to do with your partner. You're able to recognise that your state of mind just can't be trusted right now, and there is no real problem.

Because of your level of self-awareness, you don't engage or pay any attention to your low mood thinking. You walk in the door and give your partner a hug. You tell them it's good to see them, with a feeling of warmth and affection. Your partner mirrors this and reflects that feeling back at you, and the goodwill flourishes—*despite* your low mood thinking that was simmering away in the background.

Can you see how powerful this is?

Our feelings are a wonderful navigation system that is constantly giving us feedback on our current state of mind. But they are *never* giving us feedback on the truth of our reality.

Learning to check in

Once I started to see this, and I invite you to try this on for yourself, I began to build that important muscle of checking in on where I was *before* I responded.

By checking in on the feeling I was in first, I started to recognise whether I had low mood or high mood thinking. Whether my mind was racing or neutral, whether I was triggered or had clarity of mind.

It was liberating to know that I had my own internal navigation system that worked so beautifully. I just hadn't been taught how to use it effectively.

The link between thought and feeling

Low mood thinking exacerbates everything, making things look bigger and worse than they are. Understanding this gave me the patience to wait for that thinking to pass, because instinctively it made no sense to act on something that I knew was a distortion.

Once you start to see that your feelings are merely a state of mind indicator, warning your human that it's off track and it's time to press the pause button (a bit like the sensors on your car when you're reversing) the possibilities for how you can respond to anything are limitless. No more trying to work out what's going on for yourself or second guessing what's going on for somebody else.

As this became a natural way of being, I noticed I was moving through life with more ease, calm and humility. And as I was learning and getting to know the different emotional shades of myself, I stopped taking myself and life so seriously.

Realisations and insights into my funny little human started popping up everywhere:

Ah so this is how I feel when I have low mood thinking. I tend to have a lot of self-righteous thoughts, then I start justifying those thoughts until I end up believing them.

When I'm calm and patient, I never feel any sense of urgency or drama. It feels so good.

Wow this is how it feels to be neutral; I can feel this wonderful inner stillness.

For the first time in my life, I began to understand what 'looking within' truly meant, and I began to have a deep and profound experience of this.

I was getting to know myself, minus all my personal complicated thinking. But I was also getting to know my own insecure thinking and learning to be at peace with it. It was, after all, just habitual,

onary personal thinking powered by the gift of Thought and
ight to life by the gift of Consciousness.

I saw that I was just like every other funny little human out there.

We all have insecure thinking at times, we're all subject to the nature of Thought itself. None of us are broken, no one needs fixing and there is nothing to overcome.

I'll say that again because it's worth repeating.

None of us are broken, no one needs fixing and there is nothing to overcome.

The sheer relief of this for me was indescribable.

If I ever got confused about where I was in the thought cycle, and whether I had low mood or high mood thinking, all I needed to do was check in on the feeling I was in. Boom, straight away I knew what my state of mind was.

And the outward effects were huge. I became more discerning with my thinking and my own reality. I stopped believing every thought in my head, no matter how compelling. My feelings were no longer telling me how right I was, they were helping me navigate myself, my life, and my relationships with so much ease.

A story from COVID-19 lockdown

Back in early 2021, Melbourne was still deep in rolling lockdowns, and it was my birthday. It was my second lockdown birthday in a row, cut off from life as I knew it, and I was feeling flat. I couldn't go anywhere or see my extended family and friends. It didn't feel like there was much to celebrate.

My mind started mulling over how unfair it was to have another birthday in lockdown, and I began to despair that it would never end. I could really feel my mood tanking!

The link between thought and feeling

Normally, this would be the point where I would go deeper and really marinate in that mood. Or I'd swing the opposite way and start scolding myself to snap out of it, to cheer up and be grateful. Either way, I would believe every thought in my head and start wrestling with all that low mood thinking. The more I would wrestle, the more tangled up in my thinking I would become.

This time though, I had the understanding of the Three Principles on my side. I checked in on the feeling I was in and quickly realised I simply had low mood thinking. There was no problem other than the thinking I had, which made it look like there was a problem.

I gave my mind time to go quiet, I stopped looking for evidence to support my low mood. Recognising where I was in the thought cycle, and that I was simply looking through an exaggerated lens, was all I needed.

As my mind got quiet, fresh thinking came through as it always does, and my entire experience of my birthday changed. I decided to walk to a local cafe that was open for take-away, and treat myself to a lovely, socially distanced coffee. This was something I felt immediately grateful for, knowing not everyone had that luxury.

Then I had another thought to listen to some music and when I opened Spotify, one of my favourite songs that I hadn't heard in ages randomly started playing. I could feel my mood lifting and in that moment, I recognised my psychological immune system at work, doing exactly what it was designed to do—taking me from one experience to another via fresh thinking.

Instead of constantly looking outside myself and checking to see where life was in relation to me, I was now looking at where I was in relation to life.

It was so freeing to know that even if things *looked* negative, it didn't always mean there was a problem. I was simply experiencing the power of Thought in action. All I had to do was wait for a fresh thought. I didn't have to find it or manufacture it. I just had to wait for it.

Our own worlds of thought

Most of us believe that our experience of life is shaped by things happening outside of us. But if this were true, and how we felt was determined by external sources, then by that logic we would all have the exact same experience of any given thing.

We know, however, that if 10 people look at a piece of art, they may have 10 completely different reactions. This is because each person lives in their own world of thought about that piece of art that is completely unique to them. And it's not just one thought; it's the thought they have about that thought, then the thought about that thought, and so on.

No two people have the same thoughts about anything, let alone the same thoughts about their thoughts. The truth is, our entire experience is shaped by layers and layers of thought.

It's truly a world of thought.

Now, let's say I'm feeling frustrated and disconnected in my relationship. If I believe my experience comes from something outside of me, and I don't understand the difference between personal thought and the power of Thought, then I'm likely to misuse Thought against myself.

Instead of waiting for my thinking to shift or a fresh thought to appear, my mind is likely to convince me that I have only three options: control my partner, change their behaviour, or end the relationship. This leaves me powerless, because I am now reliant on something external to me (the relationship) changing before I can experience relief. There is a high likelihood that my human will start seeking comfort from the frustration and upset, in things

The link between thought and feeling

like alcohol, food, social media, or TV. As I make choices that don't truly honour who I am, the downward spiral continues.

The more disempowered we feel in our lives, the more we're governed by our insecurities and fears. But when we remember that we're spiritual beings having a human experience, and life is about the soul first and human second, we tap into a deeper understanding.

As spiritual beings, we have access to a steady flow of fresh thinking, insight, and wisdom that naturally moves us beyond the limitations of our personal thinking.

True empowerment comes from knowing that we're not at the mercy of anything outside ourselves. We're always connected to a greater intelligence that provides fresh thoughts and insights at any moment. Through this connection, our experience shifts, our thinking clears, and we remember that the power to create change comes from within.

Deeply knowing this is a soothing balm for our frightened and confused human.

The 'Fried Chicken' metaphor

Nobody likes to feel controlled or pressured to change, and we can always leave a relationship that feels unsatisfying. But if our level of awareness or consciousness hasn't shifted, and we haven't developed the understanding that fresh thinking and insights naturally come from within, then our funny little human is likely to carry the same beliefs, insecurities, and patterns into the next relationship, unknowingly creating the same issues.

A good way of looking at this is what I call the 'Fried Chicken' metaphor.

Imagine you're making fried chicken. You take a piece out of the fryer to test it and it tastes strange. You look at the chicken and think, *It must be because the chicken isn't free-range. If I use a free-range chicken instead, it'll taste better.*

So, you buy a free-range chicken, fry it in the same oil, and once again, the taste is off. This time you think, *Maybe it needs to be organic chicken.* So, you try again with an organic chicken, using the same oil, and no surprise it tastes the same.

The problem is not the chicken, of course, it's the oil. If the quality of the oil remains the same, every chicken you cook will turn out the same.

In this metaphor, the oil represents the quality of your thinking and self-awareness, while the chicken represents your relationships. Just as the oil flavours the chicken, your thoughts and awareness of your thoughts shape how you experience your relationships. When you can recognise that fresh thinking naturally bubbles up and changes the quality of your internal 'oil', you allow space for new experiences and connections.

True change doesn't happen by endlessly switching relationships (aka chickens) or forcing yourself to think differently. By looking within and recognising the quality of your thinking (aka oil), you can allow fresh thoughts and insights to come through, giving you the power to experience each relationship in a completely new, fulfilling, and satisfying way.

Chapter 10

We can't escape our humanness

Jack and Kate were married and owned a very successful business together, but they were on the verge of selling it because they were at such loggerheads with each other.

Kate liked to talk things through. It was important to her that Jack knew how she was feeling and what she was doing. This meant when her fears and worries—her human frailties—came out, Kate would tell Jack all about them. She believed this was part of being in a healthy relationship and expected him to share his feelings with her in return.

Jack, on the other hand, operated on a 'need to know' basis. If he felt something was important, he would share it, but he didn't see the point in discussing what he thought were minor things. But if Jack didn't share things with Kate that she considered important, things would soon escalate.

Kate couldn't understand why he didn't share this stuff with her. His lack of communication made her feel that she wasn't important, and she would become insecure, fearful, and angry.

Over time, Jack found Kate's desire for constant communication, overwhelming and controlling. He resented her need to know everything and so he communicated even less, deliberately keeping things from her. Sometimes he would even ignore her all together and began spending more time at work to avoid her.

With Jack and Kate's respective frailties out in full force, communication completely broke down between them and they began sleeping apart in separate bedrooms.

Understanding our human frailties

A human frailty is just an insecure thought that looks real to us in a moment of now. We all have these frailties, every single one of us. It doesn't matter how emotionally strong you think you are, how much yoga or meditation you do, how much human behaviour you study. Frailties are part and parcel of the human experience. How we handle our frailties, and the frailties of others, can have a big impact on our relationships.

When our frailties come out, the worst of us comes out with them. We can get defensive, judgemental, and project blame. We often stop listening and we start exaggerating. We shut down or we blow up. We retreat into the past to gather evidence and bring it into the now. The habitual thinking we have when we feel triggered comes to the fore. It all comes out.

There are many ways our frailties can show up. They don't go away with time, and no matter how hard you try, you can't 'personal development' your way out of them. Which means at some point in a relationship, you'll come up against your partner's frailties, and they'll come up against yours. Learning how to navigate them is a crucial part of creating thriving and connected relationships with the people in your life.

What was interesting to me when I started working with Jack and Kate, was what happened when their frailties *weren't* on display.

They each told me in their individual sessions how much they loved the other.

"She's the love of my life," Jack admitted. But I don't want to live like this. I don't know what to do". Kate would say something similar about Jack. All that love and goodwill went straight out the window the moment their low mood thinking set in and their frailties came out.

As Jack and Kate started to understand the Principle of Thought and navigating human frailties, it was like a dark cloud lifted. "I feel like the lights have been turned back on," Jack said with relief. "I now have a completely different understanding of my wife. I can see that her thinking is low, that in this state of mind she's feeling disconnected and is simply looking for reassurance."

Now that he was no longer seeing this as a negative, Jack was able to either meet Kate where she needed him or let her know when he needed time to process. In turn, Kate stopped taking it so personally when Jack would withdraw. "I can see he simply needs time, that he will get fresh thinking at some stage, that it's not on me to change his mood and the best thing I can do is give him space."

She went on. "I know now when I get that feeling of urgency that I can't trust my thinking, and I need to let my mind settle, and oh boy when my mind calms down everything looks so different! It's so freeing not to carry that emotional load anymore."

Without this understanding of the Principle of Thought, and how to handle each other's frailties, I have no doubt Jack and Kate would have separated.

The frailty minefield

When we take each other's frailties personally and get lost in our own (and then beat ourselves up for them), it impacts the connection we have with ourselves and others.

You might be someone who yells when they're upset, or you might get angry and say things you don't mean, while your partner might shut down. While this is the dynamic I see most often with my clients, the common factor here is frailty.

When we don't recognise the frailty for what it is, when all we see is how poorly someone else is behaving, we start to associate that person with their behaviour. And a couple can end up having thinking that goes something like this:

My wife always gets so angry, why does she have to be so dramatic? I hate it when she raises her voice like that. When I'm upset, I don't yell, I'm so much calmer than her. She really needs to learn how to control her temper and handle things the way I do.

I'm so over the way my husband shuts down when I try to talk to him. He takes everything I say as an attack, when all I'm trying to do is share how I feel. He always goes so quiet; nothing really gets resolved and I'm left on my own emotionally. He really needs to learn how to communicate like I do, that way we can get things out in the open and resolve them.

What do you think might happen between them here over time?

Each time their respective frailties come out, they'll see this as evidence of how different they are, and how hard it is to communicate with one another. They'll start to hold back, because it won't feel safe to share personal and intimate things with each other—more evidence of how little they have in common.

They'll start walking on eggshells around each other, because they don't have a great history of dealing with conflict. Instead, what they have is a legacy of mistrust whenever they disagree.

They'll stop feeling good around one another because all they can see are their differences. Dissatisfaction sets in and the small stuff sets them off—leaving a cup on the bench, forgetting to pick up bread on the way home, dropping a wet towel on the floor.

We can't escape our humanness

With their frailties of shutdown and anger pitted against each other, all they can see is the mounting evidence of how incompatible they are. Their poor human begins to feel completely overwhelmed and stuck.

Seeing the sameness

Now imagine if this couple understood human frailties. They would be able to see the sameness they share, through the common experience of having frailties themselves. They would see each other as human beings who simply get caught up in low mood thinking from time to time, just like every other human being on the planet.

Their minds would have the space to get quiet, allowing room for compassion and understanding to bloom. This in turn would lift their consciousness or awareness, and they would each have the benefit of fresh thinking:

I get it now, his thinking just went south, the quality of my thinking drops too. When that happens, I get really tense and self-righteous, and I feel this urgent need to express how I feel. But I know that can be overwhelming for him.

He needs time to process, so he gets quiet and goes inward and that's okay. I don't love it when he does that, but I know it's just a reflection of his state of mind right now, and the habitual thinking that comes through when he's there.

He'll come out of this when he's ready. I don't need to fix it or make it about me. He's allowed to have his experience, we all have our frailties, I get it.

You now have someone who's not as impacted by someone else's insecure thinking. They don't take the behaviour personally; they're not using it as evidence or notching it up on the list of bad deeds. They can show understanding and kindness to each other when

they need it most. Instead of getting caught up in the behaviour, they can see the frailty driving it.

Again, the ripple effects of this are huge.

You now have a couple who feel emotionally safe with one another, who can communicate and get over things quickly, and who can build a history of handling conflict well.

What's important here is recognising that frailties are a shared human experience. We all have them, and they all come from the same place, our habitual low mood thinking that looks real in a moment of now.

The light of understanding

When we can see the sameness in each other, from a genuine place of understanding, it's a whole new world for our funny little human. A refreshingly simple, less complicated world where we take things less personally.

A world where people are in their natural state, where they're loving and kind, where they get access to a higher level of consciousness, and with it the gift of choice.

When this happens the absolute best of us comes out, and relationships and people thrive.

Chapter 11

We all live in separate realities

Sarah sat across from me, her shoulders tense. "I don't understand him," she said, shaking her head. "Josh was always such a sweet, thoughtful kid. Now he's rude and dismissive, and he's always glued to his phone."

Josh was Sarah's 15-year-old son. He had recently moved up into senior school, and Sarah felt the distance between them growing day by day. Conversations were rare and often turned into arguments. Sarah's frustration was fuelled by her opinion that Josh was disrespectful and indifferent. His silence at dinner and the way he retreated to his room after school felt like rejection.

I offered an alternative view. "What if Josh isn't rejecting you?" I asked. "What if his world just looks different to yours right now?" Sarah was sceptical. "Think about what it's like to be 15," I continued. "Josh's reality is shaped by his thoughts and feelings in the moment; his need to fit in at school, his struggles with identity and his sense of independence. It's not about you. It's just what his world looks like to him right now."

Unlimited realities

It can come as a shock the first time we realise there are unlimited ways to experience something. Because it also means there are unlimited possible realities for any given thing.

Let's think about that for a moment. There are unlimited possible realities for any given thing. So, what does this mean for our funny little human?

It means that we all have different perspectives of the world. No one else has the exact same perspective that we have.

Just because something looks and sounds a certain way, does not make it so. As Shakespeare famously wrote, "There is nothing either good or bad, but thinking makes it so."[9]

As human beings, we're governed by our personal thinking, and the thinking we engage in. No two people have the same thinking, or the same thinking about their thinking. Or the same thinking about their thinking about their thinking.

There are so many layers of thought going on within all of us all the time.

Can you see how impossible it is for two people to have the exact same experience of something, given that our reality is determined by what we think, and our level of awareness, at any given moment? It seems crazy to think that our versions of the world would be the same.

Our perspective and our perception of our own reality is as unique and individual as our fingerprint. Yet so many of us live under the assumption that how we see the world is how *everyone* sees the world. We all live in a separate reality only we can see. Every single one of us.

---

[9] William Shakespeare, *Hamlet* (Act II, Scene ii, 247-9)

Separate but still connected

Separate realities are just different types of thinking, not necessarily good or bad, right or wrong, just different. No two people think alike, and being able to recognise and understand this is key to creating goodwill and good feelings between each other.

When we recognise these separate realities, we stop living in the expectation that others 'should' be able to see what we see, that our reality is all there is.

We become more humble and forgiving, because we understand there is more than one way to see something—just because it appears that way to us, doesn't mean it will appear that way to anybody else.

It's a lot like travelling to another country. I happily accept that the language, culture, and way of life there may be completely different to my own. In fact, I rejoice in and celebrate that difference. I don't expect the people there will see the world the same way I do, I simply enjoy learning about their culture and the different meanings they give to things.

But it's not so easy when someone closer to home sees things differently to us. We often take it personally and assume it's because they don't care, or they're not interested. We get offended and we judge, we blame and criticise. We keep arguing and justifying our version of reality, convinced that the way we see things is the correct and only way to see them.

We think that if they could just agree with us, if they could see things the way we do, this will make us feel better. But here's the thing, our humans don't need to see things the same way to feel close to one another. Our humans can exist in two completely separate realities and still feel close and connected.

In fact, this is happening all the time, even as we speak.

Sarah began to see that her interpretation of Josh's behaviour was filtered through her own thinking; her worries about losing connection with him and her longing for the closeness they used to share. She realised that while she saw Josh's retreat as rejection, Josh might simply see it as needing to unwind and process his day.

One evening during dinner, instead of pushing Josh to talk, Sarah decided to let the silence be. She noticed her usual thoughts rising, *He's ignoring me again, why doesn't he care?* But she let them pass and said nothing.

Later that night, Josh wandered into the kitchen while Sarah was tidying up. She resisted the urge to comment on his earlier silence and instead asked him about his day. Josh shrugged and then said, "It was okay. We had a big test in maths, I don't think I did that great."

In that moment, Sarah could see her son, not as a dismissive teenager, but a young person navigating his own challenges and insecurities. Her reality, of wanting things to be a certain way, wasn't the same as Josh's. He wasn't ignoring her or deliberately being rude, his thoughts were just consumed by high school and friends.

Recognising our distorted thinking

When we can't see that other people live in a separate reality to us, there's a lot of distortion in the way we view them.

Distorted thinking is one of those insidious things that can be hard to recognise. It looks real, it feels real, it appears as though it's coming from the other person. Our distorted thinking hoodwinks us into believing they are the one who needs to change, and that we must convince them of our point of view.

When we approach separate realities from this perspective, our human becomes critical, adversarial, judgmental, and self-righteous.

Unwittingly, what it's saying is: *My reality is the best and only reality, you need to let go of yours and accept mine.*

In other words, I am better than you, and my interests are more important than yours.

Not surprisingly, the person on the receiving end of this message no longer feels emotionally safe with us. They withhold their feelings, and they grow distant. We dig our heels in, they get defensive and stubborn, and now you have two humans playing endless rounds of emotional ping-pong, each one needing to be right and to win. This brings out the worst in us all.

Once I realised that I had a choice to bring out the best or the worst in my husband, all the criteria I thought needed to be met for us to feel connected no longer made sense.

The moment I saw through the illusion of that, I could see that we just lived in separate realities, neither right nor wrong. It was just another aspect of being uniquely human. My personal thinking fell away and a whole new world opened up for us. I stopped the fault finding. I naturally and easily had more compassion, understanding and kindness for him. And best of all, more love.

What was even more amazing though, was the way Sam responded in kind. He matched me, moment for moment. Where I showed compassion, he showed compassion. Where I showed him understanding and kindness, he showed me the same. We started to mirror each other, in the best possible way.

Our reality is as changeable as the weather

But here's the thing. Just because I can recognise our separate realities, *doesn't mean I always do.* As human beings, we move in and out of awareness of our separate realities all the time. One minute I can be living in a reality that nothing is personal and have this incredible sense of freedom and expansiveness—and the next

minute, everything is intensely personal, and everyone is wrong, and suddenly my reality is completely different. Bang, just like that.

All of which is a completely normal part of the human experience.

Like a storm cloud passing overhead and momentarily darkening the sky, the reality we each sit in can quickly change. We may move in and out of awareness, but it's still a separate reality. Not wrong. Not bad. Not even necessarily good. Just different.

How we approach our different realities can make or break a relationship. If we can approach our differences from a place of curiosity, with a desire to learn, discover and understand, our different realities will never be the problem.

But if we come from the perspective that they must be changed or worked on, our differences will become the 'reason' why our relationship breaks down.

It's not our differences that are the problem, it's the lack of understanding and accepting of our separate realities. The more we resist this truth, the more we continue to sit in judgement of each other.

Seeing the innocence in others

Once we begin to understand separate realities and recognise that they are all created by thought, and we no longer expect others to see the world the same way we do, all this space opens up.

This space allows us to be more expansive, compassionate and connected. We can be more emotionally intelligent and reflective. All of which makes us feel good; and the quality of our relationships is all determined by the quality of the feeling we sit in. It all comes down to how we feel.

We all live in separate realities

Because I know that my feelings come from what I'm thin.. when I'm in a good feeling, I know I have access to better quality thoughts. And when I've got better quality thinking, I can see that things only tend to look like a problem when my quality of thinking is poor.

When I know I can move in and out of awareness of my separate reality, and I know that my reality in the moment is dependent upon the thinking that I have, it's so much easier for me to see the innocence in another person, as well as in myself. The exact opposite of judgement and blame.

Seeing our own innocence and the innocence in others, creates an incredible opportunity for a completely different relationship. It creates space for something else to show up, minus the blame, judgement, projection, or control.

Because we can see that we are not our thinking. None of us are.

All that's happening is that we're moving in and out of separate thought-created realities all day long. Realities that look real and feel real to each of us. But once we understand that separate realities are nothing more than thought created in the moment, that they are not the only reality or the 'right' reality, that they are not who we are, they're just a reflection of where we're at, it no longer makes sense to expect someone to see things the way we do and to think the way we do.

This in turn, diffuses any discord so that we're able to adjust and pivot away from upset, judgement and blame. So many of my clients have shared with me how much lighter they feel, how much clarity they have, and how they have finally let go of the lingering resentment that had them stuck in the past.

Steve and Kelly's story

When Steve and Kelly came to work with me, they'd been separated five months after 16 years of marriage. They wanted to get back together but were stuck in an endless cycle of attack and retreat.

Steve was prone to jealousy, which would come out in frustration, anger, and upset. In his mind, Kelly wasn't making enough effort to reconcile. He was afraid she didn't love him anymore, which made him feel insecure. He would then project his upset thinking, self-righteousness and blame onto her.

In Kelly's mind, Steve was controlling and reactionary, which didn't make her feel like reaching out. When he got angry with her, she would automatically retreat until he calmed down. Her withdrawal made Steve angrier.

When I started working with them individually, one of the first things we looked at was understanding the nature of Thought and separate realities.

It had never occurred to Steve that Kelly didn't see things the way he did. It wasn't that she didn't care, she just saw things differently because she had different thinking to him. This was a light bulb moment for Steve.

He began to see that her withdrawal was more about her state of mind in that moment, which had nothing to do with her feelings for him. He could see that bringing the best out in Kelly was what truly mattered to him. He started to appreciate that his reality wasn't the only one, and that he could be okay even when they saw the world differently to each other.

Steve began to relax and feel more compassion towards Kelly. He became curious about how she saw the world, instead of making her wrong for it. He learned to check in on the feeling he was in, and this had Kelly feel safer emotionally around him. Goodwill naturally began to flourish between them.

In turn, Kelly could see that Steve's reality was completely different to hers. She began to understand that when he was upset it was because he was just lost in his thinking. It wasn't who he was, it was just where he went, and in those moments, he couldn't see things any differently.

Kelly began to feel more comfortable and confident around her husband, and stopped withdrawing every time he got upset. She was more patient and understanding of his state of mind, which enabled her to be more present with him.

This gave Kelly a sense of empowerment and self-belief she hadn't felt with her husband in years. They both started bringing out the best in one another, which created warm feelings between them. Their communication transformed, and within a month they had happily moved back in together.

This is how quickly things can change.

Without all the hard work, without rigid rules and expectations, without changing who you are. All that's required is awareness and understanding of how our funny little humans work.

Chapter 12

The truth about compatibility

Many years ago, long before I had the benefit of this understanding, a client came to me and said, "I don't get it. I was so careful about who I chose to marry. I made a list of every trait and attribute I wanted in a partner, and I held out until I met that person. When I met my husband, I couldn't believe how many boxes he ticked. But now, three years into our marriage, and he's driving me crazy!

How many of us have thought this way? That compatibility is all about boxes ticked on paper? Shared interests and values, similar personalities, and communication styles. Tick tick tick. I too believed this, until I realised that when I'm in a good feeling with my husband, I feel very compatible with him. As we talked about in Chapter 5, compatability is a feeling, not a checklist.

By comparison, when my thinking was low, I would notice our differences more. I'd go back into the past and get hung up on something that happened months or even years ago. And, funnily enough, I didn't feel very compatible with my husband when I was in that head space!

Sam hadn't changed at all; he was exactly the same person he'd been moments before. It was my thinking that changed, and with it the quality of the feeling I was in.

Compatibility has much less to do with how similar our interests, backgrounds, or personalities are, and a whole lot more to do with understanding how human beings work.

True compatibility comes from a deep connection, and the ability to navigate differences with understanding and compassion. Any relationship can thrive when both partners have a fundamental understanding of their psychological functioning. This understanding helps us to navigate challenges and maintain a loving and harmonious relationship.

Compatibility is not a static, two-dimensional trait. It's a dynamic quality that grows and evolves as couples deepen their understanding and connection. The key to lasting compatibility is not finding the 'right' partner that ticks every box, it's the ability to appreciate and love the person you're with, regardless of your differences.

Pete and Rebecca's story

Pete and Rebecca had been together for 15 years and had two children. They came to me because they were struggling to communicate and connect. They were having big blow ups on almost a daily occurrence.

Pete was someone who loved structure, routine, and a sense of order. He would get up at 4:30am most mornings to go to the gym or ride his bike. He liked being at work early and finishing his day with everything ticked off and completed. On the weekend, he'd prepare his meals for the week ahead, coach his son's soccer team and manage his daughter's tennis team. Pete was a 'doer', he loved to be busy.

What Pete did not like was change.

Now Pete's wife, Rebecca, was quite the opposite. She was someone who liked to let things flow, to see how the day unfolded. She believed in the power of taking a nap, relaxing when she needed to, and was not remotely interested in getting up at the crack of dawn to go to the gym.

Rebecca thrived on change and spontaneity, often doing things at the last minute. She loved variety and trying new things, having adventures, and generally embracing whatever life had to offer with open arms.

In the beginning, these differences were a point of attraction for them both. Rebecca admired Pete's drive and felt taken care of by his sense of order and organisation, and Pete loved Rebecca's adventurous spirit and sense of flow. That is until one day those same qualities started to drive each other crazy.

Evidence gathering

Pete started to feel irritated when his routine was interrupted, and Rebecca began to find Pete overbearing and controlling. Pete started seeing Rebecca's list of unfinished projects around the house as a weakness of character. Her general disorganisation and habit of letting things flow started to frustrate him. When they tried to talk about these issues, Pete would get angry and Rebecca would shut down.

They both wanted to feel more connected to each other, but these apparent differences and their different ways of handling them, seemed to be an impossible hurdle. Rebecca wanted Pete to slow down and be calmer, and Pete wanted Rebecca to be more organised and focused.

In other words, Rebecca wanted Pete to be more like her and Pete wanted Rebecca to be more like him.

The funny thing is, when people first get together, they usually see each other's differences as a refreshing change. They enjoy the fact that their partner has their own vibe, their own way of doing things. They like the novelty of being challenged or inspired by each other.

We're often attracted to qualities in others that we'd like to develop more within ourselves. But, as time goes on and our funny little human becomes more impacted by the content of its thinking and becomes more entrenched in its reality, the more the feeling of appreciation wanes.

Our awareness shifts, dissatisfied thinking creeps in, and we start gathering evidence to confirm this. Without an understanding of our psychological functioning, or the Principle of Thought and the role emotions play, we start thinking we're just too different and that we should be with someone more like us.

The illusion of differences

This was certainly the case with Pete and Rebecca. By the time they came to me, they were convinced they were incompatible, their differences were the problem, and these differences were looking more and more insurmountable.

Now imagine if we had focused on all the reasons why they were incompatible. They certainly had enough evidence of this and so talking about this would only have entrenched this reality even more.

Instead we talked about the nature of being human. We talked about thought and emotions and the truth of compatibility—that when a couple *feel* compatible, they *are* compatible.

Compatibility really comes down to the power of a good feeling.

Pete and Rebecca could see that when they had high mood thinking, funnily enough, they weren't focused on their differences. In fact, they were appreciative of what they each brought to the table.

Rebecca was grateful that Pete took such good care of things and was so organised. Pete, on the other hand, appreciated Rebecca's lightness and sense of fun and laughter.

The truth about compatibility

They started to recognise that the only time they seemed incompatible was when they had low mood thinking. With different thinking, came a different feeling, and a completely different experience of the same person.

Pete told me, "I love how Rebecca ignores my human when it's uptight. I know I need that, and I'm grateful to have a partner who can see this."

Rebecca agreed, "Now that I no longer trust my upset thinking, I'm having all these thoughts of how grateful I am that Pete handles the things that he does. I didn't believe you at first when you said compatibility is something that you feel, but I can see how true this is."

When we *feel* compatible, we *are* compatible. And that feeling of compatibility is just a thought away.

Chapter 13

The power of insight-based change

In her first mentoring session with me, Stephanie shared some concerns about her relationship. She and her partner were trying for a baby, but she was having doubts about whether he was the right person to have a child with. Stephanie was worried they were too different, but she was also worried about her chances of having a child if the relationship ended.

We talked about the Principles of Thought and Consciousness, and Stephanie began to look at her situation through this lens. I could feel her mind slow down and go quiet (always a beautiful thing to witness) and I was curious to see what would show up for her afterwards. Insights often follow sessions where a client has let go of the heavy mental 'thought' load they had been carrying.

At our next session, I checked in with her about her relationship, and the concerns she'd shared with me. Looking surprised, Stephanie said, "I can't believe I'm saying this, but I'm not even thinking about it at all. I have no concern about it. All the thinking I had last time we caught up; it's gone. I honestly feel like I've transcended it completely. We're really doing great."

We both laughed, and Stephanie said, "I know, my funny little human got so hung up in all that worried, concerned thinking.

And then it started looking at all the reasons why that thinking was true, and started over complicating everything, and then I just got so stuck. But after our conversation, it all just fell away, and it hasn't been on my mind since."

She added, "I love looking in the direction of these principles, it takes me out of the weeds, out of that mental noise, and all that worry and concern, and takes me somewhere else. And when I go there, my thinking is completely different. It's really quite amazing, and yet nothing has changed. He is exactly the same. It is my experience that has so fundamentally shifted."

The power of insight

When we need to make a change in our lives, most people immediately think of all the hard work and effort it will take. Change is hard, right? If it was easy, then everyone would be doing it. But when it comes to creating long term, sustainable change, it really comes down to one simple thing. The power of insight.

Insight is a profound realisation that shifts our understanding of ourselves and the world around us. It has the power to transform our awareness and elevate our consciousness in an instant, opening up choices that once felt impossible. With insight, we gain the freedom to show up in new ways and take actions that align with our true selves.

When we understand and trust in the power of insight to do the heavy lifting for us, something magical happens. The effects radiate outward in ever-widening circles, to uplift everyone around us, from individuals to families to entire communities. Change becomes effortless, natural, and deeply transformational.

Most conventional change theories and programs focus on techniques and strategies. These tools can be useful for a moment, but often have a limited lifespan. This is because they rely on application, effort, willpower, and the right mindset to keep working.

The power of insight-based change

The problem with willpower or motivation is that our moods and thoughts fluctuate. When we're triggered, tired, or caught in low mood thinking, accessing the right state of mind to apply these tools can feel impossible, leaving us feeling like we've failed.

Insight-based change is different.

It taps into something far more powerful than self-discipline. Insight comes from a deeper intelligence within us, beyond the limits of our ego and intellect. This wisdom flows naturally, lifting us to new levels of understanding without any effort on our part. When insight comes through, it doesn't just change our actions for a moment, it transforms the way we see and experience life itself.

This is the power of insight; a force that transcends temporary solutions and reveals the heart of who we are. It brings lasting change, not through effort or discipline, but through an awakening to the deeper truths within us. Once you see it, you can't unsee it. And from this place, change is no longer something we work for, it's a truth we live.

A light bulb moment

I've witnessed my clients and students experience insights so profound that it changed the physical appearance of their face. Their jawline relaxed, their frown lines softened, and the grooves around their mouth (often due to sadness or anger) faded. All the tension in their face and neck eased as their perceived limits of themselves and others fell away, and their whole approach to life shifted to a calmer, grounded and more peaceful one.

One of the earliest insights I had myself, was not long after I had come across this understanding. Sam and I were having a conversation, and he said something I didn't agree with. I looked at him, expecting to feel upset or annoyed, but instead I felt a wave of affection and attraction for him. It shocked me.

I realised I had always equated disagreement with upset. But in that moment, I could see quite clearly that disagreeing with Sam didn't mean there was a problem. It didn't mean I had to be in an upset feeling. In fact, my feeling was quite the opposite!

This was a real light bulb moment for me. The way I showed up to a difference of opinion, from that point on, changed instantly and permanently through the power of that single insight. Insights can be small and subtle. Their power lies in their impact, and a small insight can be just as powerful as a bigger one.

It's about experiencing one of those moments where something clicks inside you, revealing a completely new perspective. When you trust in the power of insight to bring this clarity, all your old, stale, and unnecessary thinking falls away, leaving you with a fresh understanding.

A new reality

When we create change in our relationships via insight, it generates a different feeling. Insights elevate us to a higher level of awareness or consciousness, and from there our reality completely changes.

Now we have access to new thinking. We've had a realisation that impacts us on a deep level, beyond our intellect. We now have a much deeper knowing and understanding.

There's a big difference between knowing something, which comes from our personal mind, and a deep knowing, which comes from a much deeper place within us. We can draw from the depth of that knowing, that insight. A funny thing about insight though; insights choose you, you don't choose them.

So, it's not so much having an insight, as it is about being in the state of mind where one shows up for you. This is part of its beauty; insight-based change takes all the burden, all the responsibility for changemaking, off our shoulders.

As human beings, we can really carry this like a heavy weight: *There's something wrong with me, I have to fix myself.* And when we're carrying this burden of change, we can get very caught up in our intellect and our personal thinking. And when we get caught up in our personal thinking, we overcomplicate things and we get stuck.

When we have the power of insight, we can trust it to do the heavy lifting for us. Change becomes natural and easy, which is a sweet relief to our overthinking little humans, burdened by the belief that they need to work on themselves, fix themselves and manage themselves to create change.

This also reflects back on our relationship with life, because when we have a deep understanding of insight, we can hand things over. We can say to ourselves, *You know what, I really need fresh thinking around this, I'd love to see this in a different way.* We can put it down because we know it's not on us, it's not up to us.

We know that insight will come because we understand the way our reality works. We understand the power of insight-based change.

Everything I'm teaching you in this book is about insight-based change. It takes the burden of responsibility for change off our shoulders, which is a breath of fresh air for our human, and wonderful for our soul.

An insight without content

Sometimes we can have what is called a 'contentless' insight. There might not be a big story or specific thought attached, it might simply be a new level of awareness or a sense of clarity that shifts how we experience life overall.

This type of insight can bring a heightened sense of peace, grounding, or connection for no particular reason. It's like waking up to a new way of seeing, where you feel lighter or freer, yet you may not know exactly why.

This is what Stephanie had experienced in her relationship. A shift, an expansion, an insight without content. She couldn't really describe the insight itself, her thinking had simply fallen away and she found herself at a higher level of consciousness.

From that higher level of consciousness, Stephanie had a completely different experience of her partner and her relationship. She had access to more philosophical thinking, and so she felt more relaxed about it. In fact, she was no longer concerned about their differences at all, something which only two weeks earlier had been all consuming.

I am always in awe of this extraordinary capacity within us all. The way our thinking can transform entirely, with no effort on our part and no clear steps on how it happened. That's the true power of insight, it sweeps through us, washing the ego clean, leaving us with sparkling clarity and a profound shift in understanding.

Choosing not to engage with our thinking

I've been fortunate enough to have had many profound realisations about my marriage, insights that have changed everything between my husband and I.

As I began to understand the Principle of Thought, I became aware of how much dissatisfied thinking I'd been bringing into my relationship. This constant stream of low-grade dissatisfaction was seeping into every aspect of how I showed up; my tone of voice, how grateful and appreciative I was, and my ability to stay present and let go of past grievances.

I realised that whenever I engaged with that dissatisfied thinking and saw it as fact rather than fleeting thought, it not only affected the way I interacted with Sam, it also affected the way he interacted with me. I wasn't seeing the best in him, so it brought out the worst in him. I was caught in a cycle of my own making, unconsciously creating the very issues I wanted to avoid.

It was a big turning point once I could see this. Engaging in my insecure, upset thinking no longer made sense. Why would I want to live in a constant state of dissatisfaction, and then bring that feeling into my interactions with my husband?

Why would I want to bring out the worst in someone I love?

The path of least resistance

The quickest path to lasting transformation is when an old pattern stops making sense.

When our emotions seem justified, they'll keep resurfacing no matter how hard we try to suppress them. When anger feels right, it locks us into a battle with ourselves, one that our funny little human will never win.

Our mind will find all the evidence it needs to justify that anger, and suddenly those feelings of frustration and resentment seem completely reasonable. In that moment, we're not just feeling our emotions, we're reinforcing them, validating them, and allowing them to spill over into our relationships.

All those feelings project outward, colouring our interactions and the way we treat the people around us. The cycle continues as our feelings seek confirmation in the actions of others, feeding the very emotions we want to escape.

When something stops making sense to us, our inner battle reinforcements just fall away. We break free from the loop of evidence-based thinking to justify our resentment or judgement. In a moment of clarity, those old emotions simply don't make sense and once that happens, they fade away. They lose their grip because we're no longer holding onto the belief that they're right or necessary. In that space, change is effortless.

It's a relief to realise that we don't have to fight our feelings; we just need to understand what they're telling us about our state of mind. When we do, our energy shifts, our outlook softens, and we become more open to seeing situations and the people in our lives with fresh eyes.

Real transformation begins, not with struggle, but with a shift in understanding.

The beauty of humility

Before I understood this deeper perspective, I had pretty rigid ideas about what a couple should share. For example, I had always imagined myself with someone who loved reading as much as I did. I pictured us lying in bed together on a Sunday morning, reading the weekend papers, talking about world events, and having deep, connected conversations as a result.

My husband Sam is a musician, and music is his passion. He has a deep appreciation for lyrics and really listens, absorbing the meaning in a way that moves him. But Sam doesn't read.

In my mind, I used to judge him for this. I would think, *How can you grow or expand your mind if you don't read?* I had a lot of dissatisfied thoughts about it. I would buy him books, only to watch them sit unread on his bedside table.

Then one day, I had a powerful realisation. I saw how deeply music moved Sam and how much it meant to him. It struck me that what I got from books, he got from music. Music shifted his awareness, his consciousness. He didn't need to read to grow, he was already doing that through the gift of music.

And then it dawned on me: Sam had never once judged me for not having a deeper connection to music, as I had judged him for not reading. He would sometimes gently ask, "Fi, do you know what that song's about?" I'd usually reply, "No, not really," as I bopped oblivious around the kitchen.

Seeing how narrow-minded I had been was humbling. I had assumed there was only one way to learn and grow, which was my way. But insight has a way of bringing us back to a place of humility.

Humility is good for the soul, and it's very good for our funny little human. It enables us to get over ourselves and step down from the high horse of our own egos. Humility is often mistaken for weakness, but it's actually one of our greatest strengths and is something the world needs more of.

Once I saw my arrogance for what it was, I felt a deep gratitude for the gift of clarity. I could even laugh at myself. I remember thinking, *Oh, Fiona, you've been so caught up in this idea that reading is the only way to grow. And here you are, with a partner who is moved by music in a way that brings such kindness, compassion, and calm to the world.*

Music is powerful. Lyrics can be poetic, profound, clever, and funny. They can break your heart, send your spirit soaring, and capture the truth of being human, everything I'd thought could only come from books. I'd been missing out on that richness because of my own inflexible view of the world.

Now, I see it so differently. I've come to appreciate the beauty and depth in music, and for that, I have Sam to thank.

When we allow ourselves to be humble and let go of rigid, narrow thinking, we open up to the possibility that our greatest teacher might be standing right in front of us. This was a beautiful realisation for me, one that deepened my appreciation for the power of insight and its transformative impact.

I know that I'm always one insight away from a completely different experience. Insights are deeply spiritual and profoundly divine; they allow us to see and experience the world in new ways, with fresh eyes and an open heart.

I feel immense gratitude for this gift. I can feel how it nourishes both my soul and my funny little human. It's a shift that goes beyond words, beyond form, bringing me back to the universal love that's within us all. Every single one of us has access to this power, and to the profound wisdom and clarity that insight brings into our lives.

Chapter 14

The gift of deep listening

Sally and Jane had been together for over 10 years. They'd recently made a big move interstate with their two-year-old to the area where Jane had grown up. Sally was struggling with the change and missed her friends and family. She felt as though Jane did not fully appreciate what she was going through.

Sally wore her heart on her sleeve. If she had something on her mind, she needed to share it and she'd get highly emotional if she didn't feel heard. Jane was more reserved and preferred to process things on her own before talking about them. She sometimes found Sally's emotions overwhelming to deal with.

Jane felt a lot of guilt about the move and Sally's struggle, but she didn't know how to make things better. They both felt disconnected, and their attempts to communicate with each other often led to arguments.

If Jane sensed an intense conversation coming, she would get anxious and grow quiet. She felt like Sally was expecting her to solve all her problems, so she felt pressured to find the answer or say the right thing. It never occurred to Jane that all Sally might need was to be heard and understood.

Sally took Jane's withdrawal personally and felt judged and hurt by what she perceived as indifference. She'd accuse Jane of not caring about her. Sally was keen to grow their family, but she didn't feel secure enough in their relationship to have another baby. She worried that another child would only magnify their problems.

The link between conflict and listening

Much of the conflict in our lives and our relationships boils down to one simple thing: our ability to listen.

All the joy, connection, and playfulness we can experience, the curiosity and wisdom we can tap into, is directly related to how well we listen and the place we listen from.

Listening is the key. As George Pransky so beautifully put it, *"Listening is the unsung hero of connection"*. When we truly and deeply listen, our relationships flourish.

The trouble is, our funny little human often misunderstands what listening is all about. It has all sorts of unspoken rules about listening, such as: *I'll only listen to you if I agree with you.* You can imagine how this gets us into trouble.

It's something most of us struggle with. We tend to be poor listeners without even realising it. To listen well requires more than simply not speaking. We need to know how to get over ourselves. We need to recognise when our mind is open and when it's not. We need to know how to navigate our thoughts and emotions, and appreciate the power of a quieter mind.

True listening is about being fully present with another human being. Once we understand how to do this, our capacity to connect expands exponentially. We can read a room, hear beyond the words, and pick up on things the speaker may not even be aware of. The sense of intimacy and connection this can generate is extraordinary.

The gift of deep listening

This is known as 'deep listening', and it has the potential to transform not only our relationships but also our experience of life itself.

Deep listening vs active listening

Deep listening is our ability to hear beyond our own intellect, ego, and logic, and move past what we agree or disagree with. It's about connecting with the essence of what the other person is truly expressing, and tuning into the deeper meaning and feeling behind their words.

With deep listening, we step out of our narrative and into theirs. It allows us to be fully present without the need to judge, analyse, or respond. It invites us into a quiet space where we can feel what they feel and see the world through their eyes. It creates a powerful bond of empathy and understanding, where words are secondary to the shared human experience.

In contrast, active listening is more focused on *how* we're listening, than what we're actually receiving. It's about whether we're nodding or mirroring the other person's tone or body language or reflecting back the words we hear.

With active listening our opinion is front and centre. We're easily distracted by the words, and we get caught up in our own filter of agreeing or disagreeing. Most importantly, our ego gets involved with thoughts like: *How can I fix this for them? What were they thinking, I would never have done that. Don't they know that all they have to do is XYZ?*

These ego thoughts have nothing to do with listening. We're too busy thinking to listen properly. We're just waiting for our turn to speak.

Deep listening means continuing to listen until it feels truly right to ask a question. And when we do ask, it's through a clear, open

lens—a lens of curiosity that says, *I will keep listening and asking until something meaningful emerges.*

From this place of openness—listening deeply, asking thoughtful questions, and staying fully tuned in to the other person—insights may begin to surface. Fresh, new perspectives can appear naturally. Until then, we remain in a space of curiosity, allowing ourselves to simply keep listening and asking, trusting that understanding will arrive when the time is right.

Once Sally and Jane began learning about separate realities and the power of deep listening, things started to shift. They became curious about each other again and they let go of the long-held assumptions blocking their connection.

Sally started to see that when Jane was quiet, it wasn't because she didn't care. Jane's human was simply caught up in low mood thinking and was fearful of saying the wrong thing. Sally could empathise with how Jane felt, recognising that she too had been trapped in her own thinking.

Sally's frustration and hurt was now replaced with compassion and a deeper appreciation. She listened through a lens of calm understanding that had been missing for years.

In turn, Jane could see that when Sally was frustrated, it was just an expression of her low mood thinking. This freed Jane from feeling responsible for Sally's emotional state. She began to trust in the power of fresh thinking and insight, knowing that Sally also had access to this natural inner wisdom.

With this new level of insight and understanding, Jane became less fearful of Sally's emotional state and found herself more open and curious about her partner. Their relationship quickly turned around. What had once seemed like insurmountable differences now appeared as nothing more than funny little human misunderstandings.

When I followed up with Jane and Sally recently, they had just welcomed their second, much longed-for child. They were both relaxed, laughing, and playful with each other. It was truly wonderful to see how far they had come.

Stepping into another person's reality

Deep listening presents us with a golden opportunity—to step into and understand someone else's reality, rather than trying to convince them of our own. When we step into someone else's world, we gain insight into what matters most to them, and from there, we know what to speak to. This naturally fosters a stronger sense of connection, as we can address their concerns, fears, or hopes in a way that resonates.

By speaking to what's real for them, we can build a bridge of empathy and compassion. With enough understanding, conflict begins to dissolve, replaced by a shared sense of humanity. After all, conflict can only exist in the absence of understanding; when we see the world through another's eyes, we create space for common ground and genuine connection to occur.

Simply repeating what someone has just said back to them, does not mean we're listening. When we deeply listen, we take the other person in. We effectively remove ourselves; we have no agenda, there's nothing to get, and no place to get to.

When we deeply listen, our mind is blank, we're not engaging with our personal thinking. Our human is in a comfortable place of 'I don't know, I don't know, I don't know' until that magical moment when something divine occurs to us and gives us a nudge. And then we might share that nudge before going back to listening and asking questions.

An act of love

There's an old saying that I think is so relevant here: 'People don't care how much you know until they know how much you care.'

When we deeply listen to another human being, they feel seen and heard. They feel loved and cared for. They feel like they matter. Deep listening is the gift of love and presence we can give to others and to ourselves. When people genuinely feel heard, they feel understood. They feel valued and connected. Their minds relax. They're open, calm, and curious— and they want to listen to you in return.

This opens the door to a profoundly beautiful exchange.

I often have my clients and students practise deep listening with each other. It brings people together in a way that problem-fixing never will.

The difference between listening and assuming

As with Sally and Jane, poor listening often leads to assumptions, which can be a real thorn in relationships and cause a lot of disharmony.

This is because assumptions are an empty knowing. When we assume something about someone, it blocks the path of understanding. Our human stops being curious. We stop listening for what's beyond the words, and we jump to conclusions. We decide we already know what our partner is saying or meaning, without actually asking.

The added problem here is that human beings tend to assume the worst. We rarely assume someone has the best of intentions; we tend to assume quite the opposite.

This can be particularly problematic in long term relationships. People reach a point where they think they know everything there is to know about their partner, and so they stop being curious or interested in the other person.

It's one of the greatest lessons I've learned, to never assume.

The gift of deep listening

By staying curious, neutral, and open, it's amazing what you can learn about another person, even if you've known them for years. There are so many doors that open for us when we deeply listen to another human being.

This is key in enabling us to see our partners, and the people we care about, with fresh eyes.

Chapter 15

Coming home to love

In a moment of beautiful synchronicity, I had a powerful conversation with a close friend the day I started writing this chapter.

She said, "Fi, I'm so tired of being hurt, tired of being mad, tired of feeling stuck. I just want to stand in my power."

I asked her what standing in her power meant to her. Without hesitation, she replied, "It means that I'm deeply rooted in my own divinity."

I paused for a moment and then said, "The only way to truly stand in your power and be rooted in your divinity is through love."

This is what coming home to love is all about; our capacity to come home to ourselves and our true nature. To generate, receive and experience love.

When I talk about divinity, I'm talking about the deeper, spiritual essence of who we are. It's the part of us that exists beyond our thinking, and beyond our ego. It's the purest expression of love, wisdom, and peace that we all have within us.

To be 'rooted in your own divinity', means to connect with that inner source, the place within you that's unshaken by life's challenges and is always aligned with love. It's where our true power lives—not in force or control, but in the quiet, steady knowing that love is our natural state.

Life, for our funny little human, is the journey of coming home to that love. It's not something we have to search for outside ourselves, but something we return to within. Every step we take, every challenge we face, is guiding us back to that source of love—our true power, our divinity.

Love is who we are

Even when we feel disconnected, disappointed, hurt, angry, or alone, coming home to love is a journey back to our wholeness. That journey relies entirely on our capacity to embrace love, especially in our darkest moments.

The more we welcome love into our lives, the richer, more fulfilling, and meaningful our experience becomes, no matter what's happening around us.

Why? Because love is who we are. That's why it feels like coming home.

At our core, we're expressions of pure, divine love—without exception. We're born with the innate knowledge of this truth, but somewhere along the way we forget. We start to believe the lie that love is something we can lose or have to earn, that our past mistakes or who we are make us unworthy of love.

But how can we lose something that is part of our very being? Love is not an object we can lose. It is the essence of creation itself.

Divine love transcends the human experience and elevates the soul. It reminds our human self that there's always a path forward, even when we can't yet see it.

A free and open mind

Our ability to embrace love is the foundation for everything in life. It's the key to experiencing joy, peace, and calm. How deeply we connect to this truth determines our ability to show up in life without the heavy emotional baggage so many of us carry.

Sydney Banks said, "Love is a mind that is free of contaminated thinking." 'Contaminated thinking' is the judgement we place on ourselves and others. It's the worry we carry about the past or the future, the unresolved anger we hold onto when life doesn't go our way. And it all blocks love from flowing through our lives.

A mind free of such thoughts is a mind that's open, present, and ready to give and receive love. It's a whole new world, one that has always been there, patiently waiting for us to notice.

Love is the foundation of the Universe. It's woven into everything around us. It's the state of mind we always return to. It's the divine gift that allows us to navigate life's ups and downs and come home to emotional and spiritual wellbeing.

Letting love in is essential for maintaining our psychological, emotional and spiritual health. The best way we can support this is to understand that love is our natural state. It's where we're meant to be; nothing and no one can take that from us.

Marie's story

On a recent Relatable call, one of my students, Marie, shared a powerful story about the changes she'd experienced.

Marie said, "This understanding took a while to fully take root, especially in how I relate to my partner. Over time, though, our dynamic has shifted dramatically, and I can see that it's because of how I'm now showing up."

She went on, "Honestly, this program was my last-ditch effort before leaving the relationship. I thought, *I've got nothing to lose, I'll give this a try.* I'd been analysing everything—our attachment styles, love languages, you name it—thinking there was some crucial piece I was missing. Now I believe what I've learned here is *it.*"

She shared a recent example, "My partner and I had a little episode last night. I could see he was caught up in a storm of negative thoughts, and I felt this lightness inside. I wasn't taking his words so seriously, and I think he picked up on that. The tension passed quickly, which is so new for us. Afterwards, he even said, 'I don't know why I say those things sometimes.' I replied, 'I know, and it's okay. You don't have to believe everything that crosses your mind.' We sat together, totally comfortable, without any lingering animosity."

Marie reflected on how they no longer get lost in the weeds during arguments. They no longer feel emotionally abandoned by each other.

She added, "I was trying to explain this to a friend, but it's hard to put into words. It's like there's a wordless place we go to, where we're no longer knocked sideways by our thoughts. The impact on us has been incredible. I've studied so many techniques, strategies, and models in my life, and I even have a PhD in Human Behaviour. But this understanding? It transcends them all."

I had goosebumps all over as I listened to her share.

Marie's story reminded me of the profound shift that happens when we truly understand how our experience of life works. She wasn't just changing her relationship; she was transforming herself.

She had moved beyond trying to 'fix' things from the top down, beyond the strategies and techniques, beyond analysing every issue. Instead, Marie was able to tap into a place of peace, where words and methods and fixing simply weren't needed.

In building her relationship from the bottom up, Marie had a foundation of understanding, presence, and self-awareness to support it. This wasn't about patching over surface problems or trying to manage behaviour; it was about creating a relationship anchored in a deeper connection.

Marie was no longer swayed by every thought she had. She had a new-found clarity that allowed her to bring out the best in herself and her partner. This bottom-up approach brought a new level of strength and resilience, a way of relating that goes beyond superficial theories, where real, lasting change begins—not just in relationships, but in how we experience life itself.

This is the power that one person has to create effortless change. This is what's possible when we understand how to build a relationship from the bottom up, on a firm foundation of closeness and understanding—which has very little to do with shared values, personality types, attachment styles, and date night fixes.

We feel good, and when our funny little human feels good, our focus and energy is on that good feeling, which creates a magic all its own.

Seeing beyond behaviour

It can be easy for our human to get caught up in the actions and behaviours of others. And when we fixate on how distant, angry, or hurtful someone is, it's an easy jump to believe their behaviour is who they are.

But what if we could see beyond their actions? What if we could recognise that beneath all the noise, there's something far deeper at play?

Our behaviour is the outward expression of how we're navigating life in the moment. Poor behaviour often stems from thoughts, emotions, or unconscious reactions that are rooted in fear, insecurity, and confusion. But our behaviour doesn't tell the whole story. Behind those human actions or reactions is something pure and untouched by the storms of thought.

That something is the essence of who we are, our divine nature, and it can get buried beneath layers of insecure thinking, frustration, and pain.

When people act out, they're caught in the trap of their own distorted thinking. They temporarily lose access to the truth of their own divine nature.

But when we can see human behaviour through this lens, it becomes easier for us to have compassion for others; even when their actions are difficult and painful to deal with. Instead of reacting to the surface behaviour, we can look deeper.

We can recognise that the person in front of us is simply lost in their own thinking, and disconnected from the love and wisdom that naturally resides within them.

We can start to see the fundamental difference between their behaviour and who they really are at their essence. We can recognise their innocence.

An important note: this is not about accepting or excusing harmful actions and behaviour.

Seeing the innocence in ourselves and others benefits *us*. Understanding that everyone is doing the best they can with the thinking they have (thinking that looks real and true in any given moment of now) helps *us*.

It releases us from the prison of anger and self-righteousness and opens the door to a sense of clarity and calm. From that higher level of awareness and consciousness, we can make decisions and choices for ourselves that feel right.

Our capacity to see the difference between how someone behaves and who they are, is the gateway to letting more love into our lives.

If we can't see the difference between them, we'll always get stuck and fixated on the behaviour, the unfairness and the victimhood, the blame and resentment. The ones who pay the price for this is ourselves. It robs us of our joy and peace and has little bearing or impact on the other person.

Recognising this is what sets our funny little human free.

It allows us to shift our perspective. Instead of getting trapped in all the frustration, judgement, and blame (the feeling of which we then live in), we can approach the situation with empathy and curiosity. We can choose to hold space for the other person. This allows room for their mind to settle and become clear.

This shift doesn't just help us respond with more love and patience; it helps us see the person for who they truly are. When we recognise the divine nature behind someone's behaviour, we stop taking things so personally. We start to see ourselves and others with more grace and understanding.

Safeguarding your inner world

I often advise my clients and students (and myself) to protect their state of mind as it is a precious resource.

Be discerning about what you allow into your mental and emotional space. Distance yourself from negativity, and steer away from gossip.

Learn to regulate your own emotions by implementing what I've shown you in this book. Recognise that not every thought you have is worthy of your attention or belief.

Don't place the burden of managing your mental and emotional wellbeing on the people around you, a common pitfall in many relationships.

Ground yourself in nature as often as you can, whether it's walking through the park, in the mountains, or by the sea. Nature has a way of effortlessly resetting both our human and our soul.

Create space in your life to simply *be,* without an agenda. This is where fresh ideas and insights bloom, and you can tap into your own clarity.

Understanding your own state of mind, means recognising when you're feeling expansive and open, and when you're feeling restricted and closed. Lean into your inner wisdom in those expansive moments and see what's fresh for you. There are no rules here, it's about tuning in and seeing what makes sense.

This is why our relationship with wisdom is so important for our funny little human. The more we allow our innate wisdom to guide us, the more open and connected we are to life, ourselves, and those around us.

Letting wisdom guide you means trusting that the answers will come, even more so when you're feeling calm. Instead of rushing to make a decision on the spot or spiralling into anxious overthinking, you can allow yourself time and grace to let your inner knowing lead the way. Wisdom shows up when your mind is quiet, helping you make choices that feel right for you.

Life isn't personal, even though it feels that way sometimes. Protecting your state of mind means recognising that there's no fixed reality. Our experience of life is fluid, shifting with the quality of thinking we have access to at any given moment.

Letting love in means seeing the innocence in ourselves and others. Our realities are all shaped by the same principles, and we are all doing the best we can with the level of awareness we have at any moment in time. If we could see differently, we would choose differently. It's that simple.

Letting love in means living from a place of grace and humility. It's about being humble during life's highs and giving ourselves grace during the lows. It's about noticing when we're caught up in our thinking, and when we're free from it. Grace is when two souls connect and everything else falls away. No judgments, assessments or rules.

Letting love in comes via the deep understanding that you are enough.

Loving yourself first

Protecting your state of mind and giving yourself grace allows you to truly see and connect with others on a deeper level, beyond the consuming and distracting noise of thought. We cannot see in someone else what we haven't yet seen in ourselves.

So, if you want to experience more love, bring it first to yourself. Breathe life into it, make it your priority above all else, and I promise you magical things will start happening in your life.

This understanding has shown me there are no limits, only infinite levels of experience. And to know that I've helped create that for myself still feels incredible, even now as I write these words. It's absolutely, fundamentally changed the quality of my life. The goodwill between my husband and I is luxurious and abundant. Our connection, trust, and attraction has soared.

I would much rather live in the feeling of the creation of love, than that of self-righteousness, judgement, and justification. And

as someone who was once addicted to feeling self-righteous and justified, this is so healing for my soul.

Take a moment to notice where you let love in your life. Notice also where you block it, and where you could generate more of it. You are the creator here. What do you commit to creating around this for yourself and the people in your life?

Turning up the love dial

At the start of last year, I decided to do an experiment.

I wanted to see just how much love I could generate in my life, and the lives of those around me. I decided I would turn the dial of love way up and see what would happen.

I didn't tell anyone in my life, except for my clients and Relatable students. I wasn't trying to get anything in return, I was simply curious to see what my human could bring to the world through love alone.

A big part of dialling up the love, is about understanding and embodying what I call the love ethic. I'll talk more about this in the next chapter, but to start, I focused on cultivating a deeper feeling of love within myself. After all, to generate something, we first need to experience it fully ourselves.

I took complete ownership of the feeling I carried within me and that I shared with others, knowing that my emotions and reactions were my responsibility and no one else's.

Too often, we inadvertently tie how we feel to external factors like other people's behaviour, expectations, or situations, all of which are beyond our control. This means that if those external factors don't meet our expectations, our mood can plummet, leaving us feeling anxious, frustrated, or disappointed. It's almost impossible to generate anything consistent or meaningful when we believe our wellbeing depends on something outside of ourselves.

Taking complete ownership over the feeling I was in, meant that if I was in a low mood, I didn't project all my upset and insecure thinking onto the people around me. Instead, I chose to go quiet and ride it out. I'd lay low until the low mood thinking and feeling had passed.

A quick note: *If you're going to go quiet and lay low, make sure you give the people around you a heads up first. Don't just disappear and leave the people in your life worried and scrambling to work out why!*

Turning up the love dial, without any expectations or agenda, brought changes that were both profound and deeply personal. I found myself letting go of resentment, justification, and defensiveness. I chose not to feed those feelings, and if they surfaced, I waited until they softened within me before I responded or reconnected.

I set an intention to acknowledge my husband in small, loving ways. When he called from work, I made sure he knew I was happy to hear his voice. I showed my affection by greeting him with a kiss hello, a hand on his arm, or leaning in next to him on the couch.

Whether it was cooking dinner, grocery shopping, filling my car with petrol, or simply being extra patient with me and the kids, I made sure Sam knew his actions did not go unnoticed. I showed my gratitude and appreciation for everything he did, and I made an effort to be more present and share a warm, positive feeling whenever possible.

We are all powerful creators

Sam noticed the shift in me and he responded in kind. I could see it in his eyes when he came home, there was a brightness and a warmth like he was seeing me with fresh eyes. We were so happy to see one another at the end of each day, spontaneously saying, "I missed you today," or "I've been looking forward to coming home and seeing you all day."

I realised that there is always more to explore, and a deeper connection to be had. By shifting the way I showed up in love, by being more intentional and mindful, Sam and I unwrapped a whole new layer in our relationship.

The effects soon rippled out beyond my immediate circle. My clients and Relatable students were inspired to try the same approach in their lives, and they too noticed profound shifts—more patience, warmer connections, and more fulfilling relationships.

There were ripples within myself too. I felt lighter and more resilient, navigating some challenging situations with a deeper sense of calm and even playfulness. Instead of my usual anxieties or frustrations, more often I felt a sense of peace and gratitude. My other relationships became smoother, and conflicts felt less daunting and were resolved faster.

The experience confirmed how powerful we are as human beings, and how capable we are of shaping our experience in remarkable ways. By choosing to show up with unconditional love, we can create meaningful change, not only in our own lives but in the lives of those around us.

Taking personal ownership of the energy we bring into the world allows us to experience real emotional freedom, deepen our connections, and find lasting fulfilment. We are powerful creators, each and every one of us. We are continually shaping our reality through the choices we make and the love we share.

Chapter 16

The love ethic

When Daniel first came to see me, he was holding onto years of resentment toward his father. "We've never been close," he said. "He's always been critical, distant, and hard to please. Honestly, I don't even know why I'm here talking about it—I don't think he'll ever change."

Daniel wasn't looking for reconciliation. In his mind, the relationship with his father was too far gone. But what he didn't realise was how much this unresolved tension was affecting him—not just in his relationship with his father, but in how he showed up in his marriage and as a father to his own kids.

"I try not to let it bother me," Daniel said. "But every time I see him, it's like I'm back to being that little kid who could never do anything right. And then I take that frustration home, and it spills over into everything else. My wife says I get short with her and the kids when I've been around him.

"How am I supposed to love someone who's been so hard on me my entire life?" he asked. It's a question many of us face in our relationships—how do we respond with love when hurt, anger, or resentment feels so justified?

The generator or the justifier

In every relationship, there'll be a time when we need to be the bigger person. Where we need to commit to what we're generating, rather than what we're justifying. The attention we bring to this is key.

To generate love, we need a strong ethic of love. What do I mean by this? Well, just as a strong work ethic is about valuing and prioritising work, a love ethic is about valuing and prioritising love.

But a love ethic is not about striving, struggling, and pushing through, in fact, it's quite the opposite. It's simply about getting out of our own way.

It's about quieting our minds and allowing our personal thinking to fall away. Knowing that when we do, we have this extraordinary, natural, built-in capacity to experience another person with fresh eyes. It's less about external effort and hard work, and more about internal, insightful understanding.

A love ethic is about deeply seeing that love is already present. It's seeing how our experience is shaped by our thinking, and how we can move toward love by raising our awareness and consciousness. It's about letting go of habitual thinking patterns, and allowing the deeper, universal energy of love to guide us and our relationships.

If your human is used to succumbing to its own insecure thinking, then your love ethic might need some strengthening. Even in moments of conflict, misunderstanding, or emotional disconnection, the power of this lies in the knowing that a simple shift in thinking can bring us back to a place of love and harmony.

When we have a rise in consciousness, we see love more clearly, free from the distortions of ego or fear. When we're operating from a lower state of consciousness, the strength of our love ethic will help shift our perception back to a more loving, understanding place.

The love ethic

The love ethic perspective also encourages forgiveness—of ourselves, our partners, and whoever we're in relationships with. By recognising that we're all living in our own thought-created realities, our human can bring more compassion and understanding towards the past, and to painful memories, mistakes, and miscommunications.

Through our work together, Daniel realised he didn't need to fix the past or force himself to feel something he didn't. He also didn't need to fix his relationship with his father. What Daniel needed to do was let go of the emotional weight he'd been carrying for so many years.

Clinging to those feelings was only keeping him stuck, limiting his ability to show up fully for his wife, his kids, and himself. By learning to quiet his mind, he let go of the stories he'd been holding onto, and as his resentment eased, he found clarity and a sense of freedom.

When Daniel stopped justifying why he couldn't move on and focused on generating love instead, everything shifted. He could see that love isn't about fixing others or excusing the past—it's about freeing ourselves to live with greater clarity and compassion in the present.

Are you generating love in your relationships?

Or are you justifying why you can't?

Opening the door

The love ethic is simple. When we let go of old patterns and quiet our minds, we create space for something new to emerge. For Daniel, this meant no longer letting his father's actions define his feelings, and instead, stepping into the freedom to create love where it once felt impossible.

Our capacity to bring compassion and forgiveness to ourselves and others and let go of hurt, pain and upset, is fundamental to our wellbeing, and the wellbeing of humanity as a whole.

The love ethic lies in understanding how to see beyond the temporary nature of our human experience and reconnect with the deeper truth of love. When we embrace the love ethic, we create ripples of change that extend far beyond ourselves. It's not about doing more—it's about being more, and letting love guide us in ways we never thought possible.

The world needs more funny little humans who are willing and open to let love in—generating love for themselves, their families, and their communities. Together, we can send out a giant wave of love everywhere we go, and watch the magic of this unfold and ripple out beyond anything we can imagine.

Conclusion

You are the creator

As we wrap up this journey together, my hope is for you to understand and appreciate your own funny little human. To embrace the fascinating, quirky, often hilarious nature of the human experience that we all get to navigate—the ups, the downs, the sideways, and all the crazy, wonderful moments in between.

Accepting and loving our own funny little human helps pave the way for a greater understanding of each other. It's the key to emotional peace, freedom, and joy.

Together we've explored the simple truths that shape all human experience; the Principles of Mind, Consciousness and Thought. We've looked at the three key relationships we're always in—our relationship with ourselves, our relationship with life, and our relationship with others.

These relationships are all interconnected, nourishing one another in an endless infinity loop, like cups continuously pouring water from one to the other. When we invest in our relationship with ourselves and with life, it naturally enhances our connection with others, opening us up to a more fulfilling, harmonious way of living.

We've looked at how Thought works and how understanding the nature of our humanity enables us to let go of the exhausting mental load so many of us carry. A load that blocks connection, intimacy, and opportunity, and can keep us stuck in the same debilitating thought patterns for years, decades, or even whole lifetimes.

When we view life solely through the lens of our human mind, everything around us—people, behaviour, circumstances—appear bigger, scarier, and more personal than they really are.

My hope is that this understanding helps you to show up to life and all it has to offer with a lightness of being. A lightness that reminds you to not take life or your human too seriously, to laugh at your own quirks, and find joy in the ordinary, everyday moments. It's the ordinary that creates the extraordinary, after all.

This journey isn't just about having better relationships. It's about honouring and celebrating what it means to be a soul experiencing life as a human. Your funny little human is doing the best it can with the thinking it has. Thinking that feels real and true in any given moment.

Nurture each of your three key relationships, and embrace these connections with openness and curiosity, because they give life so much richness and depth. They are the threads that make life so interesting, so beautiful, and so worth living.

This is the journey to emotional freedom, wellbeing, and a truly happier life.

Thank you for coming along on this adventure.

May you continue to find joy and gratitude in your all-too-human moments. Keep evolving, keep living, and savour the freedom and peace that comes from truly understanding the nature of Thought, love, and the essence of who you are.

Much love to you beautiful soul, and your own funny little human.

Fiona x

What's next?

Want to take this conversation to a deeper, more transformational level?

Introducing Relatable: My signature online program that will change the way you experience your life and your relationships forever.

Relatable takes the understanding introduced in this book and brings it into real life. Using the profound power of insight, together we explore everyday challenges and find new ways to respond to them with ease and clarity. With videos, audios, and our amazing Relatable family, as well as live Q&A calls twice a week, you'll experience this journey in real time with others on the same path.

Over eight weeks, I'll guide you deeper into this conversation, helping you see beyond limiting thoughts and tap into a creative potential within yourself—a shift that transforms not only your relationships but also your sense of wellbeing and connection.

To find out more head to this link:

fionalukeis.com.au/next-step

About the author

Fiona Lukeis is changing how we approach and understand relationships. Through her acclaimed Relatable program, weekly livestreams, and highly successful podcast, Fiona has empowered thousands of people across the globe to build deeper, more meaningful connections.

Fiona's passion for helping people inspired her to write *Funny Little Human*, where she offers fresh insights and a deeper awareness that transform how we see ourselves and those we love.

A sought-after speaker and facilitator, Fiona has led retreats and programs both in Australia and internationally. She believes that authentic, meaningful relationships are the cornerstone of a fulfilling life.

Fiona's approach to life is refreshing and down-to-earth. She understands there's no 'right way' to navigate life's complexities. Her gentle warmth, honesty, and humour make her teachings relatable and impactful.

When she's not guiding her clients and students, Fiona finds solace in nature, spending time with her husband Sam, their family, and beautiful dog Arlo.

To get in contact, email Fiona at: fiona@fionalukeis.com.au

Find out more at: fionalukeis.com.au

Thank you

To my ever-patient husband Sam, who has been at times my greatest teacher. Thank you for never giving up on me, allowing my light to shine and for being my rock no matter what.

My four children, Lachlan, Finlay, Archer, and Ciara. I love you beyond words. You inspire me every day to keep growing and moving forward.

To my beautiful sister Emma, who saved my life and believed in me time and time again, thank you.

My sibling Noa, you are the most beautiful example of what honouring yourself means. Thank you for always having my back.

My ever-supportive parents Ian and Jennifer who have been my greatest champions, and shown me time and time again that anything is possible.

To my very special friend Anthony, what a blessing it is to know you. You are the embodiment of determination, courage, service, humility, and grace.

My beautiful clients and precious Relatable students, thank you for your faith and trust. To anyone who has ever taken the time to send me an email sharing how my work has impacted them, thank you

for reminding me that no matter what, I need to keep showing up and being of service.

To every teacher and mentor I have come across and every human committed to creating change in the world, thank you for illuminating the pathway for us all.

Notes